First published in the United States of America in 1996
by Trafalgar Square Publishing, North Pomfret, Vermont 05053

**Printed in Hong Kong by
Midas Printing Ltd.**

The publisher has endeavored to ensure that all project instructions are accurate. However, due to variations
**in readers' individual skill and materials available, neither the author nor the publisher can accept
responsibility for damages or losses resulting from the instructions herein.** All instructions should be
studied and clearly understood before beginning any project.

Editors: Ljiljana Ortolja-Baird and Simona Hill
Designer: Bet Ayer

Library of Congress Catalog Card Number 96–60161

ISBN: 1–57076–062–4

· CONTENTS ·

· The
PLAYROOM

· HOUSE POCKET TIDY ·

Little people love little pockets to tidy things away, and this wallhanging
is the perfect answer. Our tidy is in bright, primary colors but you can easily substitute
the fabrics to match the decoration of a little person's own room.

Finished size 24 x 15¹/₂ in/61 x 39.4cm

MATERIALS
- 16 x 10¹/₂ in/41 x 27cm of yellow fabric for the background
- 16 x 11¹/₂ in/41 x 29cm of blue fabric for the background
- 16 x 2¹/₂ in/41 x 6.4cm of patterned green fabric for the background
- 12 x 11in/30 x 28cm of green fabric for the house
- 13 x 5in/33 x 13cm of tan for the roof
- Fabric scraps for the pocket windows, chimney pots and appliqué motifs
- 14in/36cm strip of lace for the roof edge
- 24 x 18in/61 x 46cm of fusible webbing
- 1yd/1m of ¹/₂ in/1.3cm patterned ribbon to trim the windows and door
- ²/₃ yd/0.6m of ¹/₂ in/1.3cm lacy flower ribbon for the tops of the window boxes
- 2¹/₂ yd/2.3m of 2¹/₂ in/5cm wide red binding for the borders
- 25 x 16in/64 x 41cm of pelmet weight Pellon
- 25 x 20in/64 x 51cm of backing fabric for the hanging strip and backing
- 2¹/₂ yd/2.3m of yellow ric rac braid for the border
- 14 x ¹/₂ in/36 x 1.5cm of square wooden dowel for the hanging bar
- 1¹/₄ yd/1.15m of cord for hanging

CUTTING OUT
1 To make the roof and the appliqué motifs, trace the patterns provided to make templates. Place the templates right side up on the right side of the fabric and mark an outline. Cut the required number of each shape. Cut two doors in pale blue. Make your own house number template.

2 Place the templates right side down on the paper side of the fusible webbing and mark an outline. Cut the required number of each and iron the fusible webbing to the wrong side of each shape.

3 For the three pocket windows on the house, cut six dark blue shutters 4¹/₄ x 1¹/₂ in/10.8 x 3.8cm. Cut two dark blue shutters, 2³/₄ x 1¹/₂ in/7 x 3.8cm.

4 Cut three pale blue windows 2¹/₄ x 4¹/₄ in/5.7 x 11.4cm. Cut one roof window 2³/₄ x 2¹/₂ in/7 x 6.4cm.

5 Cut three pale blue pieces of backing fabric for the windows measuring 5 x 4¹/₂ in/12.7 x 11.4cm. Cut one for the roof window measuring 5 x 2³/₄ in/12.7 x 7cm.

6 Cut three red window boxes 2³/₄ in/7cm square. Cut one window box 2¹/₂ x 2in/6.4 x 5cm for the roof window. Cut one window box 3¹/₂ x 3in/8.9 x 7.6cm for the door.

7 For the tops of the window boxes, cut six lengths of the lacy flower ribbon 2³/₄ in/7cm.

8 For the window decoration, cut three strips of patterned ribbon 2³/₄ in/7cm and six strips 2¹/₄ in/5.7cm. For the roof window, cut one strip 2³/₄ in/7cm and two strips 1¹/₂ in/3.8cm. For the door, cut one strip 6¹/₂ in/16.5cm.

9 For the window box decoration, cut six strips of lacy flower ribbon 2¾in/7cm. For the roof window, cut one strip 2¾in/7cm. For the door, cut one strip measuring 3in/7.6cm.

10 For the path, cut one strip of fabric 2¾ x 1½in/ 7 x 3.8cm. To make the gate pocket, cut a piece of dark fabric 4½ x 3½in/11.4 x 8.3cm. Cut three bars 2 x ¾in/5.8 x 1.9cm. To make the chimney pots, cut two rectangles 3⅛ x 2½in/8.3 x 6.4cm.

11 To make a hanging sleeve, cut a strip of backing fabric 13½ x 4in/34.3 x 10.2cm.

MAKING UP
Use ¼in/0.6cm seam allowance throughout unless otherwise stated.

1 To make the background, with right sides together, baste, then stitch the top of the green patterned strip to the bottom of the yellow background, and the top of the yellow background to the bottom of the blue background. Tidy the edges and press the seams out. Press the whole piece.

2 To make the roof, turn under ¼in/0.6cm seam allowance and press. With right side facing, position the lace ribbon just under the bottom edge of the roof. Baste, then topstitch in place. Trim the lace edges to the same angle as the roof side.

3 Following the instructions for bonding on page 110 and using the picture as a guide, bond the green house to the background fabric.

4 Position the roof so that the lace edging overhangs the house and bond in place. Position the chimney pots and hearts on the roof and bond in position.

5 Position the sun and bond to the background fabric. Using wide satin stitch, appliqué the sun in place.

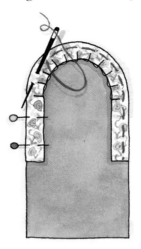

6 To decorate the pocket windows, position the decorated ribbon trim around the sides and top of all the pale blue windows. Baste in position. To attach the decorated trim to the door, gather and pleat the length of ribbon to fit around the semi-circular curve at the top of the door. Baste in place.

7 To decorate the window boxes, bond the yellow hearts to the red window boxes. Satin stitch appliqué around the outline. Turn under ¼in/0.6cm seam at the top of the red window box, baste, then stitch in place and press. Attach two lengths of lace flower trim to the top of each box for the house and just one strip to the top of the roof window box and door window box.

8 Position the window box over the lower half of the pale blue window, baste the sides and bottom of the window box to the window.

9 With right sides together, baste, then stitch the length of one dark blue window shutter to each side of the window and window box panel. Trim the edges and press the seams towards the shutters.

10 With right sides together, baste, then stitch the top and sides of the windows and door to the window backing fabric. Tidy the edges and turn right side out. Turn under a ¼ in/0.6cm seam at the bottom of the window and door and press.

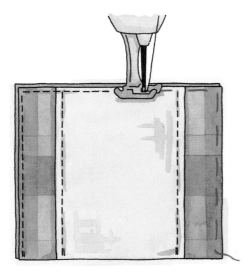

11 Position the windows and door on the house and roof and baste in position.

12 Before stitching the roof window in place, position the apex so that the window just overlaps the base. Satin stitch around the edges of the apex.

13 Machine topstitch the windows and doors down the sides, leaving the bottom of the windows and door free and the tops open for pockets.

14 For the path, turn under a seam allowance on the fabric so that the width matches the width of the bottom of the door.

15 Using wide satin stitch and matching the thread to the background fabrics, appliqué the sides and bottom

of the path, the sides and base of the house, the roof and edges of the lace trim, the base of the windows, the shutters, the chimney pots and hearts.

16 To make the gate pocket, turn under ¼ in/0.6cm seam allowance on all sides. Fold the gate in half across the width and press. Turn under a small seam allowance on the three bars and bond to the top half of the gate. Appliqué around each bar with satin stitch. With right sides together, fold the gate along the foldline and stitch the two side seams together. Turn right side out and press.

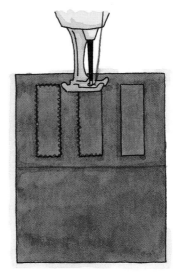

9

17 Position the gate beneath the path. Baste, then stitch the sides in place, leaving the bottom raw edge free.

18 Using the picture as a guide, assemble the birds. Bond the wing to the bird, then bond the bird to the roof. Satin stitch the legs, feet and beak. Make a dot for the eye with a blue marker pen, or use a small French knot. *(see Stitch Glossary)*

19 To stitch the tree to the house front, bond the trunk to the house, then the yellow heart to the pot. Bond the pot so that it overlaps the bottom of the trunk, then the green tree-top to overlap the top of the trunk. Satin stitch around each shape to finish.

20 To make the tidy, lay the backing fabric right side down on a clean surface. Center the Pellon and the house panel, right side up on top. Baste the three layers together.

21 Center the binding strips at each side edge of the background fabric. Baste in place, then topstitch the layers together. Position red binding strips along the top and bottom edges of the background fabric. With wrong side facing, fold the binding strips in half along the length and press. Baste, then stitch together, catching in the red binding at each end.

22 Bond your house number plate to the house above the door. Satin stitch around the outer edge and then stitch in the house number.

23 Using the picture as a guide, machine stitch ric rac braid around the binding.

24 To make the hanging strip, turn under ¼ in/0.6cm hem at the short ends of the strip and press. Fold the strip in half lengthwise with right sides facing. Baste, then stitch the length of the strip to form a tube. Turn the tube right side out and press so that the seam is in the middle at the back. Stitch the sleeve to the top edge of the tidy.

24 Drill two holes in the wooden dowel ½ in/1.3cm from each end, large enough to thread the hanging cord through. Thread the cord through the holes and knot in the middle.

10

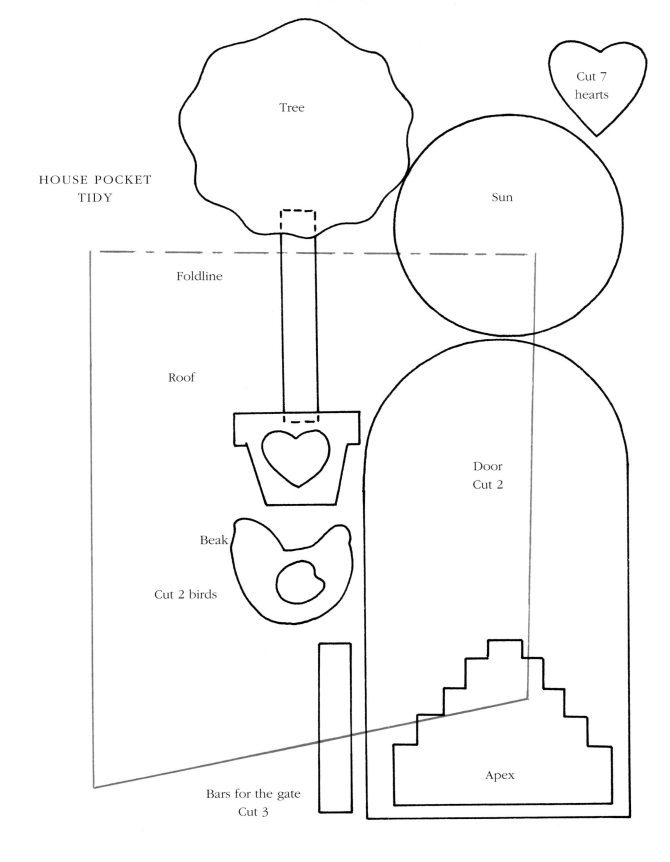

Tree

Cut 7
hearts

Sun

Foldline

Roof

Door
Cut 2

Beak

Cut 2 birds

Apex

Bars for the gate
Cut 3

11

· BUNNY RUCKSACK ·

This sturdy bag is strong enough to cope with the tugging
of even the most boisterous youngster, while the cute bunny decorations
keep their paws tightly closed over the outside pockets.

Finished size 6 x 9 x 13in/15.2 x 22.9 x 33cm

MATERIALS

- ½yd/0.5m of blue fabric with yellow spots for the background
- 1½yd/1.4m of yellow fabric for lining
- ¼yd/0.25m of red check for the flap and pocket
- ¼yd/0.25m of green check fabric for the handles and pockets
- ¼yd/0.25m of red fabric for binding the top and bottom of the bag
- ¼yd/0.25m of blue fabric for the handles
- ⅛yd/12cm of orange fabric for the carrots
- 15 x 16in/38 x 41cm of plain white fabric
- ¼yd/0.25m of pelmet weight Pellon
- 15 x 8in/38 x 21cm of 2oz batting
- Fusible webbing scraps
- Tearaway stabilizer scraps
- Velcro scraps
- Scraps of green felt
- 1yd/1m of fine cord
- One wooden bead
- Green and orange modelling clay
- Polyester fiberfill for the carrot tab
- Six buttons for eyes

CUTTING OUT

1 Trace the patterns provided to make templates for the base, flap, rabbits and carrots.

2 For the base, place the template right side up on the blue and spot fabric and mark an outline. Repeat for the yellow lining fabric and for the Pellon.

3 For the lid, place the template right side up on the right side of the red check fabric and cut one shape. Repeat this step with the yellow lining fabric.

4 For the bag sides, cut one strip of blue and yellow spot fabric 30 x 14in/76.2 x 35.6cm. Cut one strip of yellow fabric the same size.

5 For the binding at the top of the bag, cut one red strip 30 x 2in/76.2 x 5cm. For the binding at the bottom of the bag cut one red strip 30 x 1¼in/76.2 x 3.1cm.

6 For the handles, cut four strips of green check fabric, measuring 20 x 1½in/50.8 x 3.8cm. Cut four strips of blue fabric 20 x 1in/50.8 x 2.5cm.

7 For the pockets, cut two green check rectangles and one red check rectangle measuring 10 x 6in/25.4 x 15.2cm.

8 Place the carrot templates right side up on the right side of the fabric. Trace an outline and cut the required number of each shape.

9 Place the templates right side down on the paper side of the fusible webbing and mark an outline. Cut each shape. Iron the fusible webbing shape to the wrong side of the fabric shapes.

10 To make the rabbits, place the template right side up on the right side of the fabric and mark an outline. Cut six shapes, three for the rabbit front and three for

13

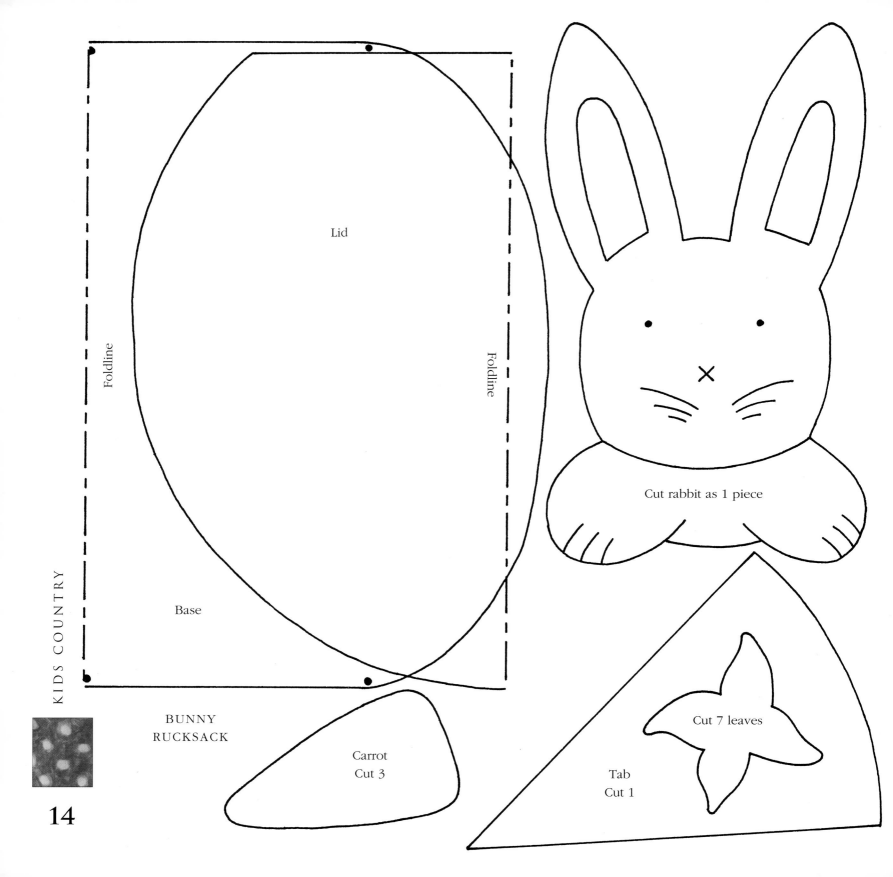

Lid

Foldline

Foldline

Base

BUNNY
RUCKSACK

Cut rabbit as 1 piece

Carrot
Cut 3

Cut 7 leaves

Tab
Cut 1

14

the rabbit back. Repeat this step, cutting three rabbits from batting.

11 Cut six inner ears for three rabbits fronts. Using the pattern as a guide, bond and satin stitch the shapes in position. Embroider the nose and whiskers. Stitch the buttons on for eyes.

12 For the flap binding, cut a strip of yellow fabric 24 x 1½ in/61 x 3.8cm.

13 For the toggle loop, cut one strip of yellow 2½ in x 1in/6.4 x 2.5cm.

14 To make the seven felt leaves, trace the pattern provided to make a template and place it right side up on the right side of the fabric. Mark an outline and cut seven shapes.

MAKING UP

1 To make the base, place the blue and yellow spot fabric right side up on the pelmet weight Pellon and baste in place.

2 Using the pattern as a guide, mark the center point on each length and the points where the curves begin.

3 Using the pattern as a guide, machine stitch through the fabric and Pellon layers in diagonal lines joining up the marked points.

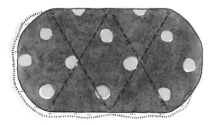

4 To make the pockets, turn under and press ½ in/1.3cm seam allowance. Fold the pocket in half across the width, so that wrong sides are facing. Mark the foldline with a pin.

5 To bond the carrot and leaf, place tearaway stabilizer at the back of each motif. Using the picture as a guide, and following the instructions for bonding on page 110, iron the carrots and leaves to the lower half of the pocket, ½ in/1.3cm from the bottom raw edge.

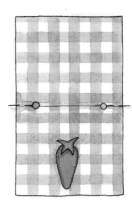

6 Using wide satin stitch, appliqué around the carrot and leaf shapes.

7 Fold the pocket in half across the foldline, and machine stitch across the top near the fold.

8 To place the pockets, use the photograph as a guide to position the pockets 1½ in/3.8cm from the bottom raw edge. Machine stitch the pockets in place, leaving the bottom edge unstitched.

9 Place the back of the rabbit right side down. On top, place a layer of batting and cover with the rabbit front, right side up. Baste the three layers together.

10 Machine straight stitch around the outline, close to the edge of the shape. Work a narrow satin stitch around the outline, so that it covers the straight stitch line.

11 Cut the excess fabric away from each rabbit outline, taking care not to cut any of the stitches.

12 Work a wide satin stitch over the top of the narrow satin stitch to completely seal the raw edges and to define the face shape.

13 Stitch a small piece of Velcro to the underside of each paw.

14 Using the picture as a guide, position each rabbit above the pocket opening on the side of the bag. The bottom of the face should align with the pocket top and the paws should act as a flap to seal the pocket.

15 Baste, then stitch the sides of the rabbit head and the top of the head between the ears in position.

16 Stitch the other half of the Velcro to the pocket in line with the Velcro on the rabbits' paws.

17 To make the handles, with right sides together, and allowing 1/4 in/0.6cm seam, stitch the length of one blue strip to the length of one green check strip. Repeat this step three times. Alternating the colors, stitch two lengths together to make a tube.

18 Turn the tube right side out and press so that the blue border strips are at each side. Repeat this step for the second strap.

19 To make the main body of the bag, mark the center and quarter points at the top and bottom of the fabric piece with pins. With right side facing, fold the fabric in half across the width, matching the pins.

20 Baste, then stitch the seam to form a tube.

21 To attach the base, with the bag tube wrong side out, the bottom uppermost, and the seam positioned in the center back, align the center points on the bag and base, and the quarter points on the bag with the center sides of the base. Pin in position.

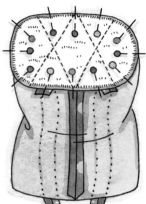

22 Place one end of each handle in position between the base and the bag sides 1 1/2 in/3.8cm from the center back seam.

23 Allowing 1/4 in/0.6cm seam, baste, then stitch the base, handles and bag tube together, catching in the raw edges of the green and red check pockets.

24 To attach the binding to the bottom of the bag, turn the bag right side out. Turn under 1/4 in/0.6cm down each side of the length of the binding and press. Machine stitch in place over the base of the pockets.

25 To make the lining, make a tube and base from yellow fabric. With right sides together and allowing 1/4 in/0.6cm seam, baste, then stitch the base to the sides. Tidy the edges and trim the seams.

26 With wrong sides facing, insert the lining in the main bag and pin in place around the top.

27 To make the flap, place the red check lid flap and yellow lining wrong sides together and baste.

28 To bind the flap, turn under ¼in/0.6cm on each side of the length of binding and press. With wrong sides facing, fold the strip in half down the length, press and slip over the raw edges of the flap. Machine stitch in place.

29 Turn under ⅛in/0.3cm seam allowance on the toggle loop. With wrong side facing fold the strip in half down the length and machine stitch together. Position the toggle loop on the underside of the flap in the center front.

30 With right sides together and allowing ¼in/0.6cm seam, position the flap in the top center back of the body of the bag, aligning the binding with the top raw edge of the bag. Baste, then machine stitch the flap and bag together.

31 To attach the red binding to the top of the bag, turn under ½in/1.3cm seam allowance along the long edges and press in position.

32 Mark the center and quarter points as for the bag. Fold the red binding strip in half across the width and machine stitch the short sides together, allowing

¼in/0.6cm seam. Tidy the edges and press the seam out.

33 Position the folded edge of the binding on the outside of the bag 1¼in/3.2cm from the top, with the raw edges of the binding turned in to the wrong side of the bag. Pin together.

34 Machine stitch the folded edge of the binding to the right side of the bag. Secure the point where the handles join the top of the bag with extra stitches.

35 Measure and mark eight evenly-spaced buttonholes around the top of the binding. *(See page 113 for further instructions on making buttonholes.)* Stitch the buttonholes horizontally, ¾in/1.9cm long.

36 Starting at the center front, thread 1yd/91.4cm of cord through the buttonholes. Slip both ends of the cord through a wooden bead.

37 To make the carrot tab, with right sides facing and allowing ¼in/0.6cm seam, stitch the sides of the carrot together, turn right side out and stuff with polyester fiberfill or scraps of batting. Work a gathering stitch around the top of the carrot to secure.

38 Place the ends of the cords in the carrot, sew securely into place. Pull the gathering stitches tight around the cord and fasten off.

39 Stitch the four felt leaf shapes to the top of the carrot, covering all the joins.

40 To make the toggle, model a carrot and leaf shape from modelling clay in orange and green respectively. Make two small holes in the center of the carrot, large enough to stitch through—use an old needle. Bake the compound following the manufacturer's instructions. Allow to cool and finish by stitching the carrot to the bag as a button.

· FARMYARD CUSHIONS ·

Farmyard animals are always popular with children. Friendly faces on squishy cushions are ideal for the tinies to cuddle up to at rest time, and the bold shapes of the design are easy to stitch.

· PIG CUSHION ·

Finished size 16 1/2 in/41.9cm square

MATERIALS
- 1/3 yd/0.3m square of green and white gingham for the pig panel
- 14 x 4in/36 x 10cm strip of yellow and white check for the corners
- 11 x 8in/28 x 20cm of yellow and white stripe for the border panels
- 11 x 10in/28 x 25cm for the blue borders
- 10 x 8in/25 x 20cm of pink and yellow spot for the pig
- Fabric scraps for the trotters, apples, leaves and stem
- 1/3 yd/0.3m of fusible webbing
- 20 x 17in/50 x 43cm of calico for the backing
- 17in/43cm square of coordinating fabric for the cushion back
- 17in/43cm of 2oz batting
- 2yd/2m of piping cord
- 2yd/2m of bias binding
- Two blue buttons for the pig's eyes
- 16in/41cm cushion pad

CUTTING OUT
1 For the pig panel background, cut one green and white gingham panel 11in/27.9cm square.

2 For the yellow and white check corners, cut four squares measuring 3 1/2 in/8.9cm.

3 For the yellow and white borders, cut four lengths 11 x 2in/27.9 x 5cm.

4 For the blue borders, cut eight strips 11 x 1 1/4 in/ 27.9 x 3.1cm.

5 To make the appliqué motifs, trace the patterns provided to make templates. Place the templates right side up on the right side of the fabric and mark an outline. Cut the required number of each shape.

6 Place the templates right side down on the paper side of fusible webbing and mark an outline. Cut the required number of each shape. Iron the fusible webbing shapes to the wrong side of the corresponding fabric shapes.

MAKING UP
Use a 1/4 in/0.6cm seam allowance unless otherwise stated.

1 To make the pig, use the photograph as a guide to position the body on the gingham panel. Following the instructions for bonding on page 110, iron the pig and trotters to the background. Position the head, the nose, the nostrils and inner ears and bond in place. Stitch on the buttons for eyes.

2 Bond the apples to the center of each yellow and white check corner, position the stem and leaf and bond in place using the picture as a guide.

3 To assemble the four borders, with right sides together, baste, then stitch one length of blue border to the long side of each yellow and white stripe border panel. Trim the edges and press the seams towards the blue border.

19

4 With right sides together, baste, then stitch one multiple blue-yellow-blue stripe border to the bottom of the pig panel. Repeat this step stitching a second border to the top. Trim the edges and press the seams towards the blue border.

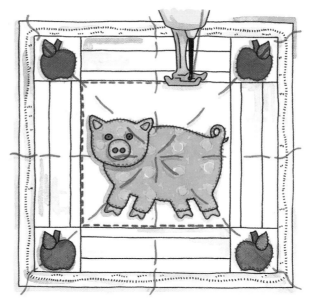

5 To attach the corners, with right sides together, baste, then stitch two corners to the remaining borders, ensuring that the apples are the correct way up. Trim the edges and press the seams to the border.

6 With right sides together, baste, then stitch the two borders to each side of the pig panel, catching in the yellow and white stripe border at each side, and ensuring that the seams meet perfectly. Press the seams towards the border. Press the panel.

7 To make the cushion front, place the backing fabric right side down on a clean flat surface. Center the batting on top, then the pig panel right side up. Baste the three layers together horizontally, vertically and diagonally.

8 Using wide satin stitch, machine appliqué around all the raw edges of the pig and apple. Using straight machine stitch, stitch over the sewing line joining the green and white gingham pig panel to the blue borders.

9 To cover the piping cord, fold the length of bias binding in half so that wrong sides are facing and press.

10 Slip the cord into the fold of the binding. Use a zipper foot on your sewing machine to stitch the binding very close to the cord.

11 Starting at the bottom center of the panel, lay the piping on the right side of the cushion front with the raw edges matching, and the fold facing the center of the cushion. Pin in position. Clip the raw edges of the binding

at the corners to make the piping more flexible. At the point where the binding starts and ends, cross the cords over each other in a V shape.

12 Using a zipper foot, stitch around the perimeter of the panel, through all the layers, close to the piping cord. Reinforce the stitching where necessary. Trim the backing and the batting close to the stitching line.

13 To make the cushion back, cut the backing fabric in half across the width. Turn under ¼ in/0.6cm seam on the raw edges that have just been cut. Turn under 1¼ in/3.2cm on the same edges. Baste, then double topstitch in place.

14 Lay out the two halves of the cushion back on a clean, flat surface, so that the hemmed edges butt up against each other. Overlap one hem over the other until the cushion back is 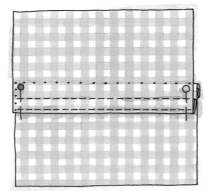 the same width as the cushion front. Pin in place, baste, then stitch the overlap together at each side in the seam allowance.

15 With right sides together, lay the cushion front on the cushion back. Baste together, then stitch very close to the piping cord using a zipper foot. Trim the edges.

16 Turn the cushion right side out and press. Insert the cushion pad.

· LAMB CUSHION ·

Finished size 16 ½ in/41.9cm square

MATERIALS
- ⅓ yd/0.3m square of blue and white gingham for the lamb panel
- 14 x 4in/36 x 10cm strip of blue and green check for the corners
- 11 x 8in/28 x 20cm of pink and white stripe for the border panels
- 11 x 10in/28 x 25cm for the green borders
- 9 x 7in/25 x 18cm of calico for the lamb

- Fabric scraps for the lamb's head, legs, flowers and centers
- ¼ yd/0.25m of fusible webbing
- 20 x 17in/50 x 43cm of calico for the backing
- 17in/43cm square of lightweight batting
- 17in/43cm square of coordinating fabric for the cushion back
- 2yd/2m of piping cord
- 2yd/2m of bias binding
- Two green buttons for the lamb's eyes
- 16in/41cm cushion pad
- Brown embroidery floss

CUTTING OUT

1 For the lamb panel background, cut one blue and white gingham panel 11in/27.9cm square.

2 For the blue and green check corners, cut four squares measuring 3½ in/8.9cm.

3 For the pink and white borders, cut four lengths 11 x 2in/27.9 x 5cm.

4 For the green borders, cut eight strips 11 x 1¼ in/ 27.9 x 3.1cm.

5 To make the appliqué motifs, trace the patterns provided to make templates. Place the templates right side up on the right side of the fabric and mark an outline. Cut the required number of each shape.

6 Place the templates right side down on the paper side of the fusible webbing and mark an outline. Cut the required number of each shape. Iron the fusible webbing shapes to the wrong side of the corresponding fabric shapes.

7 To make the Lamb Cushion, follow the instructions for the Pig Cushion. Embroider the swirls on the lamb by couching down floss before bonding to the blue and white gingham background. *(see Stitch Glossary)*

22

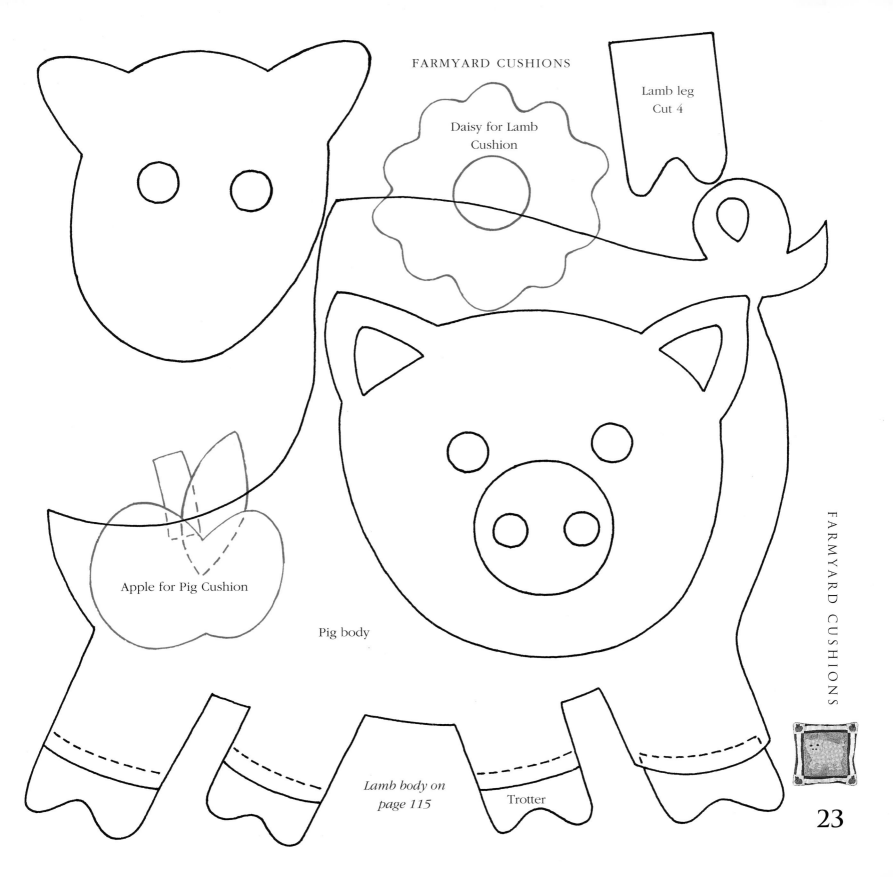

Lamb leg
Cut 4

Daisy for Lamb
Cushion

Apple for Pig Cushion

Pig body

Lamb body on
page 115

Trotter

23

· KITTEN BAG ·

This is a very simple bag to make up and suitable for carrying things out and about, or used at home for tidying toys and games. If lined with plastic instead of fabric it would make a fun bag for the beach or swimming club.

Finished size 14 x 11in/35.6 x 27.9cm

MATERIALS

- ½yd/0.5m of yellow spot fabric for the bag
- ½yd/0.5m of calico or strong cotton for lining
- 12 x 10in/30 x 25cm of blue polka dot fabric for the kitten panel
- 12 x 3in/30 x 8cm of dark check for the base of the kitten panel
- Fabric scraps for the kitten and appliqué motifs
- Ribbon ⅓yd x 1¾in/0.3m x 4.5cm for the panel top
- Ribbon ⅓yd x 1¼in/0.3m x 3.2cm for the panel base
- One strip of strong material or webbing 28 x 4in/ 71 x 10cm for the handles
- 12 x 10in/30 x 25cm of fusible fleece for lining
- Scraps of fusible webbing

CUTTING OUT

1 To make the kitten background, cut the blue polka dot fabric 12 x 10in/30.5 x 25.4cm.

2 Cut the dark check fabric 12 x 3in/30.5 x 7.6cm. Cut one length of fusible webbing to the same size.

3 To make the appliqué motifs, trace the patterns provided to make templates. Place the templates right side up on the right side of the fabric and mark an outline. Cut each shape.

4 Place the templates right side down on the paper side of fusible webbing and mark an outline. Cut each shape.

5 For the bag shape, cut one back and one front 14½ x 12in/37 x 30.5cm. Use the template on page 26 for the bag bottom and corners.

MAKING UP

1 With a hot iron, and following the instructions for bonding on page 110, fuse the dark check fabric to the bottom of the blue polka dot background.

2 Using the picture as a guide, assemble the kitten and the flowers on the background fabric. Bond the kitten body, markings, features and face markings in place. Position the leaves and the stem so that the stem just overlaps the leaves and bond in place. Bond the flower head in place so that it overlaps the stem.

3 Following the manufacturer's instructions for fusing, iron the fusible fleece to the back of the panel. Allow to cool.

4 Satin stitch around all the raw edges of the shapes. Satin stitch the mouth in place.

5 To make the bag, turn under 1¾in/4.5cm at the top edges and press.

6 Match the center of the bag front with the center of the kitten panel. Position the panel 1½in/3.8cm from the folded top of the bag. Baste the panel to the bag.

7 Position the ribbon strips at the top and bottom and baste in place. Satin stitch around each raw edge of the ribbon and down each side of the kitten panel.

Press along dotted lines

Seam allowance included along this edge

Corner of
front and
back Kitten
Bag only

8 Open out the folded seam at the top of the bag. With right sides together, and allowing ½ in/1.3cm seam, baste, then stitch the side seams and bottom seam together and press.

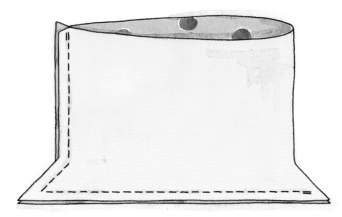

9 To stitch the corners, match the center side seam with the center of the V at the bottom. Stitch right across the seam and reinforce the stitching. Press and trim the seams to ¼ in/0.6cm.

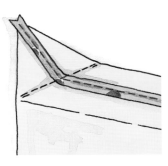

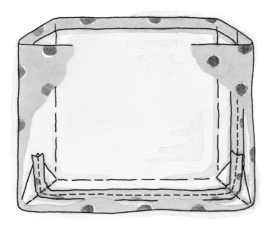

10 To make the lining, repeat steps 5–9, turning under an extra ½ in/1.3cm at the top edges. Trim the folded edge to 1in/2.5cm deep.

11 To make the handles, cut the length of webbing into two equal lengths. Turn under ½ in/1.3cm on all edges. Press. With wrong sides together, fold each length in half and press. Topstitch around each edge.

12 Position the handles on the inside of the bag top, 3½ in/8.9cm in from the side seams and down inside the bag 1½ in/3.8cm. Baste in place.

13 With wrong sides together, fit the lining in the bag to within ½ in/1.3cm of the top, and align the seams and the corners. Pin in place. Fold the top raw edge of the bag front over the lining and slipstitch together.

· TABLETOP TENT ·

Finished size covers a 31in/78.7cm square table, 28in/71.1cm high. Adapt the top and side measurements to fit your table.

MATERIALS
- 3yd/2.75m of strong calico or cotton for three sides
- 1yd/1m strong yellow stripe cotton for the entrance side
- 1yd/1m strong green and white gingham for the top
- 1yd/1m blue stripe fabric for the front of the tent
- 24 x 18in/60 x 46cm red check for the door
- 16 x 4in/41 x 10cm of white to make the windows
- 1yd x 5in/1m x 13cm yellow check for the canopy edge of the roof
- 1yd x 4in/1m x 10cm green check for the grass
- 10½yd/9.5m of 1½in/3.8cm wide bias binding
- 1yd x 6in/1m x 15cm of blue for the water
- 24 x 9in/60 x 23cm green for the window frame
- 24 x 2in/60 x 5cm green check for the window box
- Large fabric scraps for the appliqué motifs
- 4yd/3.7m of ½in/1.3cm wide ribbon for tying
- 10in/25cm of ⅛in/0.3cm wide ribbon for the hay bale
- 2yd/1.8m fusible webbing
- Embroidery floss

CUTTING OUT

1 For the top, cut one piece of green and white gingham 32in/81.3cm square.

2 For the sides, cut three pieces each 32 x 28½in/81.3 x 72.4cm.

3 For the entrance side, cut one piece 1yd x 28½in/91.4 x 72.4cm. Cut this piece in half vertically to give two pieces 18 x 28½in/45.7 x 72.4cm.

4 For the appliqué panel, cut one piece of blue stripe 32 x 28in/81.3 x 71.2cm.

5 For the grass, cut one strip of green check 32 x 4in/81.3 x 10.2cm.

6 For the water, cut one strip 32 x 5½in/81.3 x 14cm.

7 For the window box, cut one strip 12 x 2in/30.5 x 5cm.

8 For the window frame, cut one rectangle 10¼ x 8¼in/26 x 20.1cm. On the wrong side of the fabric, mark 1¼in/3.2cm in from each raw edge and join up the points. Cut the center panel out, leaving the frame.

9 For the curtains, cut two rectangles 6½ x 3½in/16.5 x 9.5cm.

10 For the window, just showing between the two curtains, cut a strip 6½ x 2in/16.5 x 5cm.

11 For the canopy, cut a strip 32 x 4¾in/81.3 x 12.1cm. Scallop one long edge using the pattern.

12 For the door, cut the red check in half to make two 9in/22.9cm widths.

13 Cut the 16 x 4in/40.6 x 10.2cm window into four 4in/10.2cm squares.

14 To make all the appliqué motifs, trace the patterns provided to make templates. Place the templates right side up on the right side of the fabric and mark an outline. Cut the required number of each shape.

15 Place the templates right side down on the paper side of the fusible webbing and trace an outline. Cut the required number of each shape. Using a hot iron, bond the fusible webbing to the wrong side of the fabric shapes. Peel off the backing paper.

16 Cut the 4yd/3.7m length of ribbon into four equal lengths.

17 Cut the 10½yd/9.5m length of bias binding into four equal lengths.

MAKING UP

A ¼in/0.6cm seam allowance is used throughout unless otherwise stated.

1 To make the picture, iron fusible webbing to the wrong side of the canopy. When cool, using the photograph as a guide, position the fabric, fusible webbing side down on the right side of the blue stripe background. Following the instructions for bonding on page 110, fuse the canopy to the background. Using a wide satin stitch, machine appliqué along the scallop.

2 In the same manner, position and bond the grass to the background, 14½ in/36.8cm below the appliquéd edge of the canopy. Then position the water directly beneath the grass with the raw

edges touching. Using wide satin stitch appliqué along the join of the two raw edges.

3 For the window frame, turn under and press ½ in/1.3cm seam allowance around the outside edge. Position the window frame ¾ in/1.9cm below the satin stitch edge of the canopy and an equal distance from each side edge. Pin in place.

4 To make the curtain-window-curtain panel, with right sides together, baste, then stitch one long edge of a curtain to the side of the window. Repeat, stitching the second curtain to the other side of the window. Tidy the edges and press the seams out. Position the curtains in the frame, tucking the raw edges under to the back of the frame. Satin stitch around the outside and inside edges of the frame and down the seams where the curtain meets the window.

5 Center the window box 2in/5cm below the bottom of the window frame and pin in place.

6 Using the photograph as a guide, assemble the flower shapes, stalks and leaves, tucking the edges of some of the leaves and stalks behind the window box. Tuck the top of the stalks behind the flower heads and leaves. When

the shapes are assembled and overlapping in the correct places, fuse each shape, including the window box to the background fabric. Use wide satin stitch to appliqué around every outline. Make a spiral shape on the yellow center of each white flower using machine satin stitch.

7 In the same way, assemble the mother hen and chicks and bond to the background fabric. Satin stitch around each raw edge. Work one French knot for each eye. *(see Stitch Glossary on page 114)*

8 Position the bale of hay, and bond it to the background fabric. Position ⅛ in/0.3cm ribbon horizontally and vertically across the center of the bale and stitch in place. Satin stitch around the raw edges.

9 To make the cat motif, using the picture as a guide, position the markings on the cat body and head and bond in place. Embroider the eyes and features on the cat face. Position the cat's body on the bale, then the head on the body and bond together. Appliqué around the body, head, and markings. Define the hind leg and ears with satin stitch.

10 Position, bond and satin stitch the rabbit, duck, ducklings, bird on nest, bees and butterflies.

11 To complete, on a clean, flat surface lay out 1yd/1m of calico, right side down. Position the appliqué panel right side up on top. Trim the calico and appliqué panel to 28in/71.1cm deep and 31in/78.7cm wide. Pin the two layers together. Trim the two bottom corners, to round the edges. At each side, position one ribbon length for tying, 13in/33cm from the top edge.

12 To prepare the binding, turn under the raw edges down each side of the length and press. Fold the binding in half down the length so that the turned under edges are together on the inside, and press. Slip

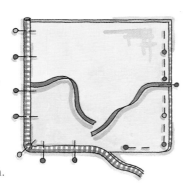

one length of binding over the raw edges of the calico and appliqué panel, on the two sides and bottom only. Ease the binding around the bottom corners as you work. Machine topstitch.

13 To make the entrance flap, using the picture as a guide, position the two sides of the door right side up on the right side of the yellow and white stripe background. The bottom raw edges of the door should align with the bottom raw edges of the background, and the side of each door should align with the inside edge of each piece of background. Bond the pieces together. Using wide satin stitch, machine appliqué over the raw edges around the top and side.

14 Position the four windows, then bond two to each side of the red door. Satin stitch around the raw edges.

15 In the same manner, bond and appliqué the door knob and the milk bottle in place.

16 Turn under a ¼in/0.6cm hem down the edges of the two door panels and press. Turn under a further

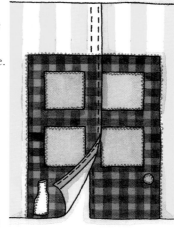

1in/2.5cm down the same edge, press, baste, then machine topstitch in place.

17 With right sides face up and the door edges meeting, overlap the left edge over the right edge so that the width of the whole panel measures 31in/78.7cm. Double topstitch the yellow stripe fabric where the two pieces overlap, from the top down to the door. Reinforce the stitching just above the door. Trim the length to 28in/78.1cm.

18 Place the ribbon ties, then bind the three edges, following the instructions in step 12.

19 To make up the tent, trim the two remaining edges to 31in/78.7cm wide and 28cm/78.1cm deep. Place the ribbons, then bind the side panels and bottom, as in step 12.

20 With right sides together, baste, then stitch the top edge of the appliquéd front to the green gingham square. Tidy the edges and press the seams out. Repeat this step, stitching the entrance panel to the right of the appliqué panel. Stitch the remaining two sides to the gingham top.

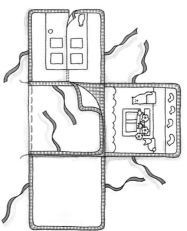

21 Reinforce the stitching in all the corners with a triangle of stitches.

· RABBIT PUPPET ·

Children never tire of inventing their own stories for play, and puppets help develop their imagination. This friendly rabbit character could be made and multiplied into a whole family.

Finished size 12in/30.5cm tall

MATERIALS

- Scraps of calico or strong cotton for the head, paws, ears and waistcoat
- 5in/13cm of checked cotton for the body
- 1yd/1m of 1in/2.5cm wide bias binding
- Scraps of stiff iron-on Pellon interfacing
- Two buttons for eyes
- Two buttons for the waistcoat
- Embroidery floss
- Scraps of fusible webbing

CUTTING OUT

1 Trace the patterns provided to make templates. Place the template right side up on the right side of the fabric, draw the outline and cut the required number of each shape.

2 Place the rabbit head, ear and paw templates right side up on the interfacing and trace an outline. Cut the required number of each shape.

3 Place the nose, inner ear and inner paw templates right side down on the paper side of the fusible webbing and mark an outline. Cut two of each shape. Using a hot iron, bond the fusible webbing to the wrong side of the fabric ears and paws.

MAKING UP

1 To prepare the binding for the waistcoat, turn under and press a 1/4 in/0.6cm seam allowance along the long edges. Fold the binding in half lengthwise, with wrong sides together and press.

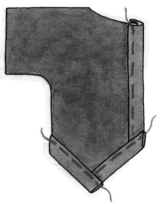

2 To make the waistcoat, slip the binding over the raw edges of the waistcoat front and cut to size. Turn under the short ends and baste, then stitch in place. Repeat this step to bind the bottom edge of the front and back waistcoat pieces. Attach a pocket flap to the right-hand waistcoat piece. Bind the neck edge on the fronts and back. Stitch the buttons in place. For a small child use appliqué or embroidery.

3 Using 1/4 in/0.6cm seam and with right sides facing, baste, then stitch the two shoulder seams together, then the two side seams. Bind the cuff of the sleeves, turning under a small seam allowance at the overlap before stitching in place.

4 To prepare the rabbit, fuse the inner ears to the right side of each front ear, and the inner paws to the front of each paw. Fuse the nose using the pattern as a guide. Appliqué around the outlines with a narrow satin stitch.

5 With right sides together, and allowing a small seam, baste, then stitch around the ears leaving the bottom short edge open. Avoiding the stitching line, clip the seam allowance around the curved edge. Turn right side out.

6 Using the template as a guide, embroider the features to the front of the head using long stitch for the whiskers and mouth. *(see Stitch Glossary on page 114)* Stitch the buttons on for eyes.

7 Position the ears on the right side of the face, with raw edges together and the tips of the ears pointing towards the neck edge of the face. With right sides facing, baste, then stitch the head front and back

together, leaving the neck edge open and catching in the bottom of the ears. Avoiding the stitching, clip the curved edges of the seam allowance around the edge. Turn right side out and press.

8 To make the paws, with right sides together and using ¼ in/0.6cm seam allowance, baste, then stitch one front to one back, leaving open the cuff edge. Trim the seams and press.

9 To make the body, with right sides together and using ¼ in/0.6cm seam allowance, baste, then stitch the side and shoulder seams together, avoiding the neckline, the cuffs and the bottom of the body sleeve. Tidy the edges and press the seams out. Clip the curved edges on the seam allowance and under the arms to make the shape more flexible.

10 Place the head inside the body sleeve upside down, so that the raw edges of the neck on the head and the raw edges of the neck on the body sleeve are matching. Ensuring that the head is facing the front of the sleeve, baste, then stitch around the neck. Tidy the seams.

11 In the same manner attach each paw to each cuff.

12 Turn right side out and slip binding around the raw edge at the bottom of the body sleeve. Baste, then machine topstitch in place. Fit the waistcoat over the sleeve and secure with stitches.

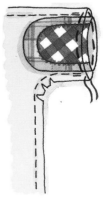

33

· CALICO RAG DOLL ·

A rag doll is a popular traditional toy. There is usually one favorite that becomes a constant companion and accompanies a child into adulthood. This tiny doll, made with love, could become an heirloom of the future.

Finished size 9 1/2 in/24.1cm

MATERIALS
- 1/4 yd/0.25m of calico for the doll
- Fabric scraps for the clothes
- Small amount of polyester fiberfill
- Two skeins of yellow tapestry wool for the hair
- Two small buttons for the eyes
- Three small buttons for the dress

CUTTING OUT

1 Trace the patterns provided to make templates.

2 To make the body, place the template right side up on the right side of the calico and cut a front. Reverse the template and cut a back.

3 In the same way cut a back and a front for the shorts from fabric scraps, a back and a front dress panel and a collar.

4 Cut two 6³/₄ x 1in/17.2 x 2.5cm strips for the appliqué border on the dress.

5 Using the template provided, cut two circles from calico for the head.

MAKING UP

1 To make the body, place right sides together and allowing 1/4 in/0.6cm seam, baste, then stitch around the edge of the body. Leave the neck open for turning.

2 Turn right side out and press.

3 Through the opening, stuff the legs. Stitch across the point where the leg becomes the body. Use the pattern as a guide.

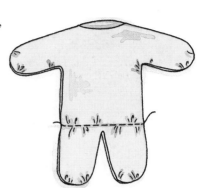

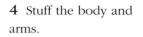

4 Stuff the body and arms.

5 Turn under 1/4 in/0.6cm seam allowance at the neck opening and slipstitch the neck edges together.

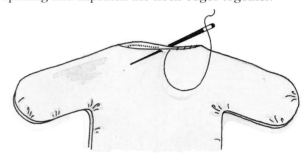

6 To make the shorts, with right sides together and allowing 1/4 in/0.6cm seam, baste, then stitch the sides and the inner legs. Tidy the edges, press the seams out and turn right side out.

7 Turn under 1/4 in/0.6cm hem at the bottom of the shorts and slipstitch in place. Turn under 1/4 in/0.6cm at the waist opening and press. Work a gathering stitch around the waist, but do not fasten off the thread.

8 Pull the shorts onto the body. Gather the thread to fit the waist and secure the ends.

35

9 To appliqué the dress border, turn under ¹⁄₄ in/0.6cm seam allowance and press. Using the photograph as a guide, position the top edge of the band 1in/2.5cm above the raw edge of the dress and appliqué in place using slipstitch.

10 With right sides together, and allowing ¹⁄₄ in/0.6cm seam, sew side and underarm seams and shoulders. Tidy the edges and press the seams out. Turn under ¹⁄₄ in/0.6cm at the wrists and lower dress edge and slipstitch. Turn the dress right side out and press.

11 To make the head, place right sides together, and allowing ¹⁄₄ in/0.6cm seam, baste, then stitch around the outside edge, leaving an opening at the base large enough to fit the neck edge of the body into. Clip the seam to ease turning. Turn right side out and press.

12 With an indelible marker pen, draw on the mouth and nose. Draw heart shapes for the cheeks and color in with a red pen or appliqué fabric shapes.

13 Stitch the buttons on for eyes, using the pattern as a guide.

14 To make the hair, satin stitch a fringe across the forehead with yellow tapestry wool. Cut the remainder of the skeins into 16in/40.6cm lengths. With the center of the lengths level with the center of the head, lay four lengths side by side across the head  and couch down. In the same manner cover the back of the head three-quarters of the way down. Couch the strands down the center back. Working from the fringe over the ear level, down towards the center back, couch the hair down in a diagonal line. Braid

the lengths of hair and tie ribbon in a bow to secure the loose ends.

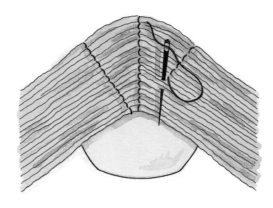

15 Stuff the head as fully as possible. Turn under ¹⁄₄ in/0.6cm seam at the base and sew the head to the body. Reinforce stitches across the join to secure.

16 To attach the collar, tuck the top raw edge over the neckline of the dress and oversew.

17 Using the photograph as a guide, decorate the dress front with buttons, stitching one at the center of the collar.

The NURSERY

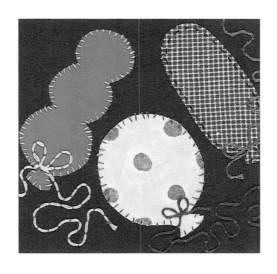

· PLAYMAT ·

This is a really large playmat that will give hours of fun.
It would make a stunning throw or car quilt and is just the thing for picnics or the beach.

Finished size 45in/114.3cm square

MATERIALS

• 20in/51cm of 45in/114cm wide plain red fabric for the checkerboard and tulips
• 13in/33cm of 45in/114cm wide red and white check fabric for the checkerboard
• 13 x 32in/33 x 81cm of plain blue for appliqué borders
• 13 x 32in/33 x 81cm of green and white spot for appliqué borders
• 8 x 16in/20 x 41cm of yellow check fabric for the corner pieces
• 8 x 16in/20 x 41cm of blue check fabric for the corner pieces
• One length of 32 x 5in/81 x 13cm of plain yellow for the borders
• One length 46 x 6in/117 x 15cm of red and white spot for binding
• Scraps of cream calico for the mother duck
• Fabric scraps for the wings, feet and cockerel's head, beaks, tail and comb
• Fabric scraps for the flowers, chicks, and cockerel, allow 4in/10cm square for each
• 1¹⁄₃yd/1.20m of calico or sheeting for backing
• 1¹⁄₃yd/1.20m of 2oz batting
• Fusible webbing scraps for appliqué motifs
• Tearaway stabilizer scraps for appliqué motifs

CUTTING OUT

1 To make the checkerboard, cut out 13 plain red and twelve red check squares measuring 6½in/16.5cm.

2 To make the inside border, cut the length of yellow fabric into four strips 1¼in/3.2cm wide.

3 To make the blue and green appliqué borders, cut two blue and two green panels measuring 6½ x 31in/16.5 x 78.7cm.

4 To make the appliqué motifs, trace the bird and flower patterns provided to make templates. Place the templates right side up on the right side of the fabric scraps and mark an outline. Cut out the required number of each motif.

5 Place the appliqué templates right side down on the paper side of the fusible webbing and mark an outline. Cut out the required number of each shape. Repeat this step using tearaway stabilizer.

6 To make the corners, cut two 6½in/16.5cm squares from each piece of yellow check and blue check. Press each square across the diagonal, and cut two triangles.

7 Cut the red and white spot binding fabric into four strips measuring 1½in/4cm wide.

MAKING UP
Use ¼in/0.6cm seam allowance throughout.

1 To make the checkerboard, with right sides facing, stitch the red and red check squares into rows of five, alternating the squares. Tidy the edges and press the seams out. Stitch the rows together to form the checkered center panel. Tidy the edges and press.

2 With right sides together, stitch one length of yellow fabric to the top of the checkerboard. Repeat this step at the bottom of the panel. Tidy the edges. With right

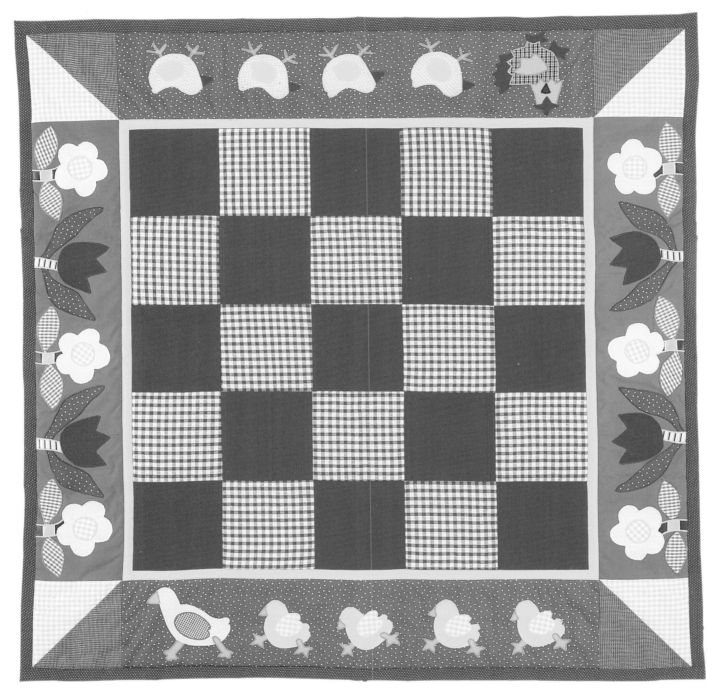

sides together stitch the two remaining yellow strips to each side of the checkerboard panel, catching in the ends of the yellow strips at the top and bottom. Tidy the edges and press the seams out.

3 To make the appliqué borders, following the instructions on page 110 for bonding, iron the fusible webbing shapes to the wrong side of the corresponding fabric pieces.

4 Assemble the pieces on each border using the picture as a guide. Place tearaway stabilizer behind each and bond the pieces to the background fabric.

5 Appliqué around all the pieces using satin stitch.

6 To attach the borders, place right sides together and baste, then stitch the two side borders to the center panel. Tidy the edges and press the seams out.

7 To make the corners, with right sides facing, baste, then stitch one yellow check triangle to one blue check triangle across the diagonal to form a square. Tidy the edges and press the seams out.

8 With right sides facing, baste, then stitch one square to each end of the remaining top and bottom corner borders. Tidy the edges and press the seams out.

9 With right sides facing, baste, then stitch the top and bottom borders to the panel. Tidy the edges and press the seams out.

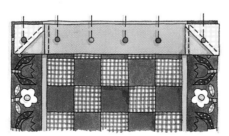

10 Trim away any excess fabric to make a complete square.

11 To assemble the playmat, spread the backing out right side down on a clean, flat surface. Place the batting on top, then center the playmat right side up on the batting to form a sandwich.

12 Baste the three layers together horizontally, vertically and diagonally.

13 Machine quilt around the yellow border and the checkerboard, quilting in-the-ditch.

14 Trim the backing and batting to the same size as the quilt front.

15 To prepare the binding, turn under and press ¼in/0.6cm seam along each long edge. Fold the binding in half lengthwise and press. Open the binding out.

16 With right sides together, baste, then stitch one length of binding to one side of the quilt front, without stitching through the batting and backing fabric. Repeat this step for the opposite side. Trim the ends to match the length of the top and bottom panels. Tidy the edges and press the seams out.

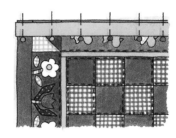

17 Repeat this step for the top and bottom panels, catching in the binding at each side.

18 Machine quilt in-the-ditch around the binding, through all the layers, and around all four sides.

19 Fold the binding over to wrong side of the quilt and baste. Slipstitch in place.

PLAYMAT

Daisy leaf

PLAYMAT

For daisy and tulip see page 121

Cut 2 legs

41

· CRIB QUILT ·

This is a super bright crib quilt to tuck well in and around the child. It would work well in a stroller to keep winter winds at bay, or on a car-seat and it could even be used as a playmat. The strong, visually stimulating shapes will fascinate a tiny tot!

Finished size 21 x 26in/53.3 x 66cm

MATERIALS
- ½yd/0.5m of plain red fabric for borders and binding
- ⅔yd/0.6m of plain blue fabric for borders
- 14 x 7in/36 x 18cm of plain yellow fabric
- 14 x 8in/36 x 20cm of plain green fabric
- 18 x 22in/46 x 56cm of green and white gingham for the border and corners
- 18 x 22in/46 x 56cm for the border
- 18 x 6in/46 x 15cm of green and white spot for the center panels
- 18 x 6in/46 x 15cm of blue and white spot for the center panels
- Large fabric scraps for the appliqué motifs
- A terry cloth scrap for the rabbit's tail
- 24 x 29in/61 x 74cm of calico for backing
- 24 x 29in/61 x 74cm of 2oz batting
- ¾yd/0.7m of fusible webbing
- Embroidery floss

CUTTING OUT

1 For the center panels, from the blue and white spot fabric, cut three blocks 5½in/14cm square. Repeat this step using the green and white spot fabric.

2 To make the yellow and the block borders, cut six strips measuring 5½ x 1in/14 x 2.5cm and six strips 6½ x 1in/16.5 x 2.5cm in each color.

3 To make the plain blue and green borders, cut six strips measuring 6½ x 1in/16.5 x 2.5cm and six strips 7½ x 1in/19.1 x 2.5cm in each color.

4 For the inner red border, cut two strips 14½ x 1¼in/36.8 x 3.1cm and two strips 22 x 1¼in/ 55.9 x 3.1cm.

5 For the striped border, cut six strips 13½ x 1½in/ 34.3 x 3.8cm, two in green and white gingham, two in orange and white stripe, and two in plain blue.

6 Cut six strips measuring 22 x 1½in/55.9 x 6.4cm, two in green and white gingham, two in orange and white stripe, and two in plain blue.

7 To make the corners, cut four rectangles, measuring 3¼ x 2¾in/8.3 x 7cm, two in yellow and two in green and white gingham.

8 To make the appliqué motifs, trace each shape from the pattern provided to make a template. Place the template right side up onto the right side of the fabric and mark an outline. Cut each shape.

9 Place the templates, with the exception of the sun's face, right side down on the wrong side of the webbing. Mark an outline. Cut each shape. Iron the webbing to the wrong side of each fabric shape.

10 For the binding, cut two strips of plain red measuring 44 x 2½in/111.8 x 6.4cm, and one strip measuring 30 x 2½in/76.2 x 6.4cm.

MAKING UP

Use ¼in/0.6cm seam allowance throughout, unless stated otherwise.

1 To make the rabbit, place the body on the green spot background fabric, using the picture as a guide. Following the instructions for bonding on page 110, iron the shape to the background. Appliqué  around the shape and the paw and hind leg markings with satin stitch.

2 Bond the inner ears to the face and appliqué around each shape. Embroider the face markings with two strands of floss using stem stitch. Bond the eyes and stitch a single French knot in the center. *(see Stitch Glossary)* Place the head in position on the body and appliqué around the outline. Bond the tail to the body and appliqué.

3 To make the butterfly, bond the wing to the background fabric and appliqué. Bond the flowers, flower centers and circles to each side of the wing and appliqué. Bond the body in place and appliqué around its outline. Make the antennae using satin stitch.

4 To make the sun, place the rays on the background fabric, using the picture as a guide. Bond in position and appliqué around the outline using satin stitch.

5 To make the face, using three strands of embroidery floss, stem stitch the nose and mouth. Bond the eyes and heart-shape cheeks in place and appliqué with satin stitch. Turn under a 1/4 in/0.6cm seam allowance around the circle and slipstitch in position. Using two strands of embroidery floss, work a small running stitch around the face of the sun, 1/8 in/0.3cm from the edge.

6 To make the watering can, assemble the pieces using the picture as a guide. Tuck the seam allowances of the top and side handles, and the spout under the body. Pin in place. Remove the body of the can and bond the handles and spout to the background. Avoiding the points of joining to the can, appliqué around the outside edges using satin stitch.

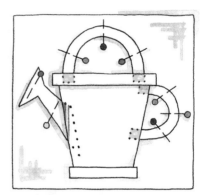

7 Replace the body, covering all the seam allowances and bond in place. Satin stitch to finish.

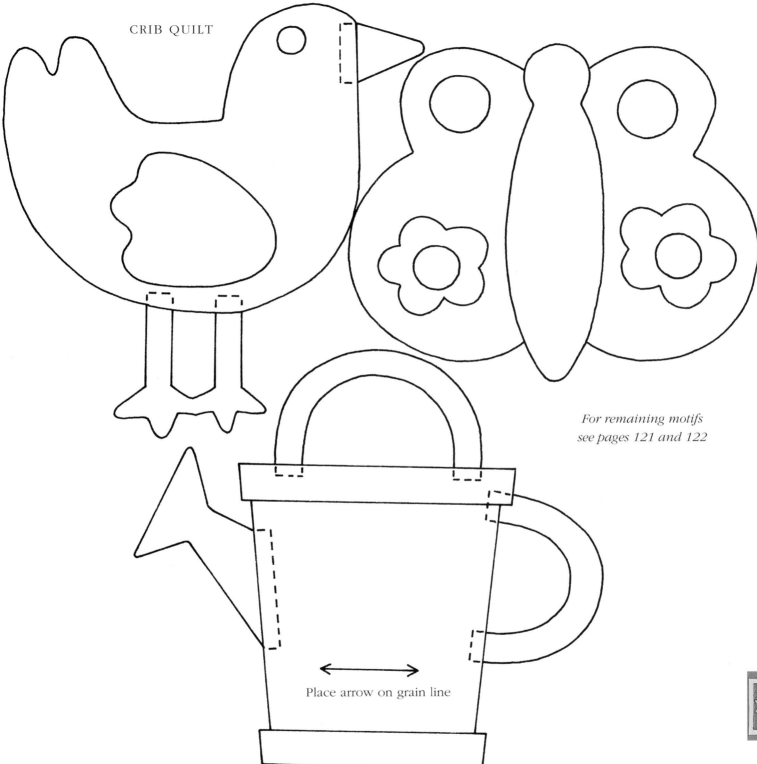

CRIB QUILT

*For remaining motifs
see pages 121 and 122*

Place arrow on grain line

45

8 To make the bird, using the picture as a guide, bond and appliqué with satin stitch, the wing and the eye in place. Assemble the pieces using the picture as a guide. Tuck the top of the legs under the body and the bottom of the legs under the feet. Tuck the beak just under the front of the face. Pin the pieces in position, then remove the body to leave everything else in place. Bond the leg piece and beak to the background and appliqué with satin stitch, avoiding the points at which the legs join the body and feet, and the beak joins the face.

9 Bond the body to the background so that it covers the seam allowances on the beak and legs. Appliqué in place. Satin stitch to finish.

10 To make the flower pot, bond the flower pot rim to the pot. Assemble the pieces on the background fabric using the picture as a guide. Tuck the stem under the pot rim and under the tulip. Tuck the leaves just under the stem. Bond and appliqué the stem in position first, then bond the leaves and tulip.

11 Bond the pot over the bottom of the stem and appliqué the sides and bottom first, then the rim.

12 To attach the red block border to the green and white spot appliqué panels, with right sides together, baste, then stitch the 5½ in/14cm strips to the top and bottom of the blocks. Tidy the edges, then press the seams out to the red strips.

13 Repeat for the 6½ in/16.5cm strips, stitching them to the sides of the block and catching in the red strips across the top and bottom.

14 Repeat for the remaining two green spot panels with red borders and the three blue and white spot panels with yellow borders.

15 Repeat to attach the blue border to the red border

and the green border to the yellow border.

16 To stitch the panels together, with right sides together, baste, then stitch the rabbit panel to the butterfly panel; the sun to the watering can; and the bird to the tulip. Tidy the edges and press the seams out.

17 With right sides together, baste then stitch the bottom of the rabbit and butterfly panel to the top of the sun and watering can panel. In the same way stitch the top of the bird and tulip panel to the bottom of the sun and watering can panel. Tidy the edges and press the seams out.

18 To attach the inner red border, with right sides facing, center one red strip measuring 14½ in/36.8cm across the top of the panel. Baste, then stitch in place. Repeat this step at the bottom of the panel.

19 Attach the side red borders in the same way. Trim the edges and press the seams out.

20 To make the striped border, with right sides together, baste, then stitch one 13½ in/34.3cm length of orange and yellow stripe to the same size length of plain blue fabric. Repeat this step stitching the green and white gingham to the plain blue. Tidy the edges and press the seams out.

21 Repeat this step for the three remaining 13½ in/34.3cm lengths and for the 22in/55.9cm lengths, so that you have four panels of color made up of three different fabrics.

22 Cut each 13½in/34.3cm panel across the width into six even blocks of three colors measuring 2¼in/5.7cm long.

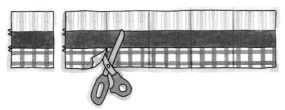

23 With right sides together, baste, then stitch the top of one block to the bottom of another block, so that each panel is made up of 18 stripes. Unpick the last stripe, to leave 17 stripes. Trim the edges and press out the seams. Repeat this step for the remaining 13½in/34.3cm length.

24 Cut each 22in/55.9cm panel across the width into eight even blocks measuring 3¼in/8.3cm. Baste, then stitch the top of one block to the bottom of another, so that each panel has 24 stripes. Unpick the last stripe so that the panel has 23 stripes. Trim the edges and press out the seams.

25 To attach the top and bottom striped border to the inner red border, with right sides together, baste, then stitch the shorter lengths of striped panels to the top and bottom of the inner red border. Trim the edges and press the seams towards the inner red border.

26 To make the corners, cut each 3¼ x 2¾in/8.3 x 7cm rectangle across the diagonal into two triangles. With right sides together, baste, then stitch one yellow triangle to one green and white gingham triangle across the diagonal. Repeat this step for the three remaining corner rectangles. Trim the edges and press the seams out.

27 With right sides together, baste, then stitch one corner to each end of the striped side border panel. Trim the edges and press the seams out. Adjust the seam allowance on the rectangles if necessary to alter the length to fit.

28 To assemble the quilt, lay out the backing fabric, right side down on a flat, clean surface. Center the batting and the quilt panel face upwards on top to create a quilt sandwich. Baste the three layers together horizontally, vertically, diagonally and along the edges. Trim all layers even.

29 To make the binding, join the three red binding strips with a diagonal seam and press open. With wrong sides facing, fold the entire length of the strip in half down the length and press. Turn under the raw edges to the center and press. Turn under ¼in/0.6cm seam at one short end and press.

30 With right sides together, match the raw edges of the binding to the raw edge of the quilt. The fold of the binding should be facing the center of the quilt. Working from the bottom left side of the quilt, baste, then stitch the binding to the quilt to within ⅝in/1.6cm of the top border. Miter the corner following the instructions on page 111.

31 Continue to bind each edge and miter each corner until the entire quilt is bound. Overlap the beginning and end of the binding by 1in/2.5cm. Fold the binding back over the stitching line to the back of the quilt and press. Slipstitch in place, covering the line of machine stitching and mitering each corner.

32 To finish, hand quilt around the outside of each appliqué motif ⅛in/0.3cm from the outline. Hand or machine stitch over the stitching line of each seam on all the borders and the center panel. In a similar way, quilt random blocks in the striped outer border.

· BIRD WALLHANGING ·

A pretty birdhouse complete with birds! They could all be bluebirds, songbirds or mocking birds. Ours are bright and stuffed, with characters of their own.

Finished size 11 x 15in/27.9 x 38.1cm

MATERIALS
- 12 x 9in/30 x 23cm green cotton for the house
- 1/3yd/0.3m square of check fabric for the roof
- Fabric scraps for the birds and the appliqué motif
- Felt scraps for the red circles on the roof line
- 1/3yd/0.3m piece of ric rac braid
- Eight buttons for decoration
- Small amount of batting for the birds
- Fusible fleece for the bird motif in the center of the house
- Scraps of fusible webbing
- Embroidery floss
- A selection of small beads and buttons
- Strong thread for hanging

CUTTING OUT

1 To make the birds, trace the bird shape from the pattern provided to make a template. Place the template right side up on the right side of the fabric scraps and mark an outline. Cut twelve bodies, wings, legs and eyes. Cut 24 feet and six beaks.

2 Place the body, wing and eye templates right side down on the wrong side of the fusible webbing and mark an outline. Cut out each shape.

3 To make the legs, cut out twelve strips of stripe or check fabric measuring 1½ x 1in/3.8 x 2.5cm.

4 To make the roof, trace the pattern provided to make a paper template. Place the template right side up on the right side of the fabric and mark an outline.

Flip over the template and mark the reverse outline on the fabric for the back of the roof. Cut each shape.

5 Cut the felt circles 1½ in/3.8cm in diameter. Cut a straight line ½ in/1.3cm across the top of the circle, so that each has a flat edge to butt up to the roof edge.

6 To make the center appliqué motif, trace the patterns provided to make a template. Place the right side of the template on the right side of the fabric and mark an outline. Cut out each shape.

7 Place the two largest circle templates, the bird, the wing and the eye right side down on the fusible webbing, trace each outline and cut the required number of each shape.

8 Trace the template provided to cut seven heart shapes from fabric and fusible webbing.

MAKING UP

1 To make the birds, iron the fusible webbing to the wrong side of each fabric shape. Turn under 1/8 in/0.3cm around the wing and eye pieces and position on the bodies using the pattern as a guide. Following the instructions on page 110, bond the wings and eyes to the bodies. Using slipstitch appliqué the pieces.

2 To make the legs, fold the stripe fabric in half down the length, so that the wrong sides of the fabric are facing. Turn under the raw edges to the wrong side and slipstitch together.

49

3 Turn under ⅛ in/0.3cm around the feet pieces and with wrong sides facing slipstitch the feet together, leaving a small opening at the top to insert the leg. Insert ¼ in/0.6cm of the leg in the foot opening and hand stitch in place. Repeat for the second leg and foot.

4 With right sides facing, baste a front and back body together. Position the legs on the body and baste in place. Stitch around the bird, catching in the legs and leaving an opening under the tail. Turn the bird right side out. Tidy the edges, press.

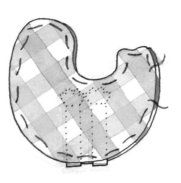

5 To stuff the bird, ease the filling into the bird, ensuring that it is evenly distributed. Slipstitch the gap together.

6 Turn under and press ⅛ in/0.3cm around the circle for the beak. Clip into the center of the circle and form a cone shape by overlapping one edge over the other. Stuff the beak and slipstitch to the bird shape.

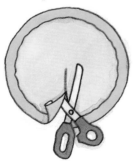 

7 To make the roof, with right sides together, and allowing ¼ in/0.6cm seam, baste, then stitch the sides and top. Tidy the edges and turn the roof right side out. Press. Turn under ¼ in/0.6cm at the bottom of the roof and press. Pin to hold.

8 To make the house, with right sides facing, fold the green fabric in half across the length. Allowing ¼ in/0.6cm seam, baste, then stitch the two sides together. Tidy the edges. Turn the house right side out and press. With the openings placed at the top and bottom, topstitch vertical lines 1in/2.5cm apart to resemble wooden slats.

9 Insert the top of the house just inside the roof, positioning it in the center so that 1½ in/3.8cm of the roof overlaps the house at each side. Baste, then stitch in place. Machine topstitch the roof and house together.

10 Using the picture as a guide, place the flat edge of the red circles across the base of the roof so that they overhang the house. Baste, then slipstitch in place. Position the ric rac braid over the top edge of the circles and overlap the roof of the house by ½ in/1.3cm at each side. Slipstitch in position and secure the edges at the back of the roof. Embroider a small stitch in contrasting floss in each zigzag of the ric rac braid.

11 Stitch a button in the center of each red felt circle.

12 To make the appliqué motif in the center of the house, iron fusible webbing to the two largest circles. Turn under 1/8 in/0.3cm and press. Bond the largest circle to the center of the green house and then bond the second circle to this. Slipstitch around the edges of the circles to secure. Couch embroidery floss around the two outer edges.

13 Cut a circle of fusible fleece 1/4 in/0.6cm smaller than the smallest fabric circle. Fuse the fleece to the wrong side of the circle and then turn under 1/4 in/0.6cm seam allowance. Baste to hold in place.

14 Turn under 1/4 in/0.6cm on the yellow bird's nest and press. Place the nest on one edge of the smallest circle with the outside edge of the nest overlapping the circle. Fold the excess nest fabric underneath the circle and baste, then slipstitch in place.

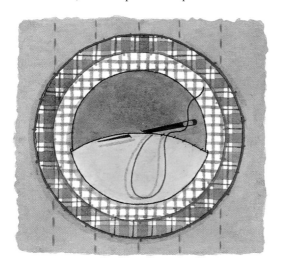

15 Place the circle right side up in the center of the circles on the house front. Baste, then slipstitch in place.

16 Bond the wing to the bird. Slipstitch around the wing edge and couch down embroidery floss to resemble feathers.

17 Bond the bird to the center of the circle. Add the eye and the beak using the same technique.

18 For emphasis, stitch a small button or use a French knot over the appliqué eye.

19 Iron fusible webbing to the wrong side of the seven hearts. Turn under a small seam allowance. Using the picture as a guide, position the heart shapes at the bottom of the lines running down the house. Pin, then slipstitch in position.

20 Using the picture as a guide, stitch one bird to the center of the top of the roof.

21 Stitch lengths of embroidery floss to the top of the heads of two birds. Slide a colored bead onto the thread. Stitch each bird loosely to the red felt circle at each end of the roof, so that it hangs on a 1in/2.5cm length of embroidery floss. Thread the embroidery floss back down through the bead and into the back of the bird. Fasten off.

22 Repeat this step, attaching embroidery floss to the center back of the remaining three birds.

23 Using the picture as a guide, space the birds evenly and stitch to the bottom of the house.

24 To hang the birdhouse, make two 4in/10.2cm lengths of string or twine into loops and stitch to the back top corners of the roof. You could make a hanging sleeve if preferred.

· RABBIT DOLL ·

This is the simplest of stuffed toys, a joy for tiny hands, and if stuffed with polyester fiberfill he will go safely through the washing machine. Leave off the button trims for young children.

Finished size 10 1/2 in/26.7cm tall

MATERIALS
- 1/4 yd/0.25m of calico for the head and body
- Fabric scraps for the jacket and shorts
- Polyester fiberfill
- Two buttons for the eyes
- Two buttons for the jacket
- Embroidery floss
- 1yd/1m of 1in/2.5cm binding for the jacket
- 8in/20cm of fine elastic for the waist on the shorts
- Small scraps of fusible webbing for the inner ears
- 1yd/1m of binding

CUTTING OUT
1 Trace the pattern pieces to make templates. Place the templates right side up on the right side of the fabric and mark an outline. Cut the required number of each shape.

2 Place the inner ear shape right side down on the paper side of the webbing and cut two. Using a hot iron, fuse the webbing to the wrong side of the fabric.

MAKING UP
Use a 1/4 in/0.6cm seam allowance throughout unless otherwise stated.

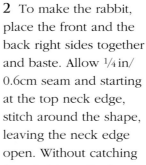

1 To make the back of the rabbit's body, with right sides facing, at the center seam, baste, then stitch the two pieces together, above and below the points marked "leave open to turn inside out".

2 To make the rabbit, place the front and the back right sides together and baste. Allow 1/4 in/ 0.6cm seam and starting at the top neck edge, stitch around the shape, leaving the neck edge open. Without catching the stitching, clip the seam allowance at the curves to make the shape flexible.

3 To make the ears, using the picture as a guide, position the inner ears on the right side of the outer ears and appliqué around the inner ear outline with satin stitch. Match each front ear to a back ear. With right sides together, baste, then stitch the curved edges together, leaving the bottom short edge open for stuffing and turning. Clip the top curved edge in the seam allowance to make the ear flexible. Turn each ear right side out and stuff evenly.

4 Using the pattern as a guide, embroider the features using backstitch. Stitch buttons on for eyes and a small felt circle for the nose. Position the ears on the right side of the head front with raw edges together and the tip of the ears facing the neck edge of the face. The inner ears will face the features. Baste in place.

5 With right sides together, baste, then stitch the two pieces of the head back together down the center seam. Press the seam out and trim the edges. With right sides together, baste, then stitch the front head to the back head, leaving the neck edge open and

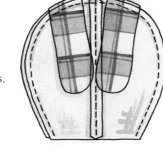

sandwiching the ears in between. Reinforce the stitching over the ear joins. Without catching the stitching, clip the curved edges of the seams.

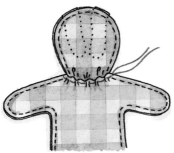

6 Work a gathering stitch around the neck opening. With right sides together, position the base of the head in the neck of the body. Align the side seams with the front of the body. Pull up the gathering thread and stitch the body and head together securely. Turn right side out and stuff evenly with polyester fiberfill.

7 Sew up the back seam using ladder stitch.

8 To prepare the binding, turn under ¹/₄ in/0.6cm seam allowance down each side of the length of binding and press. With wrong sides together fold the strip in half down the length and press. Cut the binding to size and position the fold over the front raw edges of each jacket piece and the front neck. Baste, then machine topstitch in place. Attach two small pieces for pocket flaps.

9 With right sides together, baste the jacket front pieces to the back at the shoulder seams and stitch. Bind the cuff edge of the sleeves, turning in ¹/₄ in/ 0.6cm seam at the overlap.

10 Stitch the fronts to the back at the side and underarms. Clip the seam allowance at the underarm curves and overcast all the seams.

11 Bind the lower edge of the jacket, turning in ¹/₄ in/ 0.6cm at each edge.

12 To make the shorts, with right sides together, baste, then stitch the outside leg seams. Press the seams open. Baste, then stitch the inside leg seams. Match the two legs together at the waist to the inside leg seam, and baste, then stitch the two legs together working from the center back waist to the center front waist. Trim the edges and press the seams open.

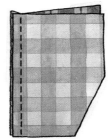

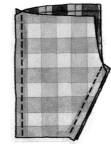

13 Turn under a ⁵/₈ in/1.6cm hem at the waist, baste, then stitch together, leaving a small opening at the center back. Thread the elastic through the opening, stitching the two ends together. Slipstitch the opening to close. Turn under a small hem at the bottom of each trouser leg and then stitch together.

· CLOTH BOOK ·

Cloth books are fun for the little tots and are virtually indestructible! We have made a book of six pages but using the same techniques you could add as many as you wish.

Finished size 7 1/2 x 5 3/4 in/19 x 14.6cm

MATERIALS
- Twelve pieces of fabric in plain and check fabrics 8 x 7in/20 x 18cm for the pages
- Fabric scraps for the appliqué motifs
- Oddments of gray felt for the mice tails
- Shiny pink or white fabric for the cake topping
- An assortment of beads and buttons for eyes and decoration throughout
- Strands of stiff cotton floss for the mice whiskers
- One skein of orange tapestry wool for the braids
- Small lengths of 1/8 in/0.3cm ribbon for the girl's braids
- 1/2 yd/0.5m of 1 1/2 in/3.8cm ribbon to bind the spine and to tie the book
- Embroidery floss
- Scraps of fusible webbing
- 8in/20cm of ric rac braid
- Fabric marker pen

NOTE: *For a young child substitute French knots for beads and appliqué shapes for buttons.*

CUTTING OUT
1 Cut twelve pages 8 x 6 1/4 in/20.3 x 15.9cm, six in plain fabric and six in patterned fabric.

2 Cut two circles, one slightly larger than the gingerbread man and one 1/4 in/0.6cm larger again.

3 Make templates from the patterns provided. Place the templates right side up on the right side of the fabric and mark an outline. Cut the required number.

4 Place the templates right side down on the paper side of the fusible webbing and mark an outline. Cut the required number of each shape. Using a hot iron, fuse the webbing to the reverse of the fabric shapes.

MAKING UP
1 Using the pattern as a guide, position one fabric number on each plain piece of fabric page.

2 Peel off the paper backing and following the instructions for bonding on page 110, iron to fix the numbers in place.

3 Appliqué around the numbers using stab stitch or around the inside edge using running stitch.

4 On each numbered page, using a fabric marker pen, write out the word for each number, underneath the appliqué number.

Couch down stranded embroidery floss over the written letters using two strands of a contrasting color. *(see Stitch Glossary on page 114)*

5 On the last plain page, write out a message such as *Happy Birthday xxx* and couch the thread down.

6 To make the picture pages, using the patterns as a guide, assemble the motifs towards the right-hand side of each page.

2 two

3 three

4 four

5 five

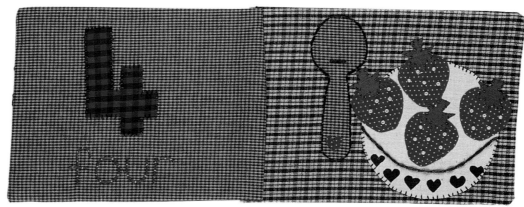

Birthday Girl

7 To make the birthday girl, bond the red cheeks then the nose to the face. Work a running stitch around the cheeks and nose. Backstitch the mouth.

8 Bond the collar, then the face to the background fabric so that the face overlaps the collar. Work running stitch along the top edges of the collar at each side and around the curve of the face.

9 Couch down a length of embroidery floss around the bottom curved edge of the collar.

10 To make the braids, cut the tapestry wool into two 12in/30.5cm lengths. Machine stitch across one end of each length to bind the strands together. Divide the strands into three sections and braid to within 1in/2.5cm of the end. Tie a bow at the end of each braid.

11 Position the braids at each side of the face. Place the crown over the top of the head, covering the stitched braid ends. Bond in place using a hot iron. Work a row of running stitches down each side of the crown. Couch down embroidery floss around the points of the crown. Stitch a bead to each point. Baste a length of red ric rac braid along the bottom edge of the crown so that it partially covers the face and couch in place.

12 Stitch two blue buttons for eyes and one green button for decoration on the collar.

Gingerbread Man

13 To make the gingerbread man, bond the largest circle to the background fabric. Center the smaller circle on top and then the gingerbread man in the middle and bond in position.

14 Around the circumference of the largest circle couch down a length of embroidery floss. Work a running stitch around the inside edge of the smallest circle. Stab stitch around the outline of the gingerbread man. Stitch in place buttons for the eyes and nose, and three buttons down the body for decoration. Backstitch the mouth and couch down embroidery floss in a zigzag pattern on the arms and legs.

Mice

15 To make the mice, bond the inner ear pieces to the mice. Assemble the mouse, tucking the tail under the body. Bond the mice to the background fabric. Work a running stitch around the inside of the inner ear and down the center of the tail. Stab stitch around the edge of the mice.

16 To make the whiskers, tuck 2in/5cm lengths of bristles or strong threads through a red bead. Stitch both the bead and whiskers firmly to the nose of the mouse. Stitch on a flat gray button for the eyes.

Balloons

17 To make the balloons, bond the shapes to the background fabric. Work a running stitch around the inside edge of one balloon and stab stitch around the other two.

Strawberry Plate

18 To make the strawberry plate, bond the dish to the background fabric. Using the picture as a guide, bond the strawberries to the dish and the leaves to the

57

strawberries. Bond the blue hearts to the edge of the dish. Bond the spoon to the background fabric at the side of the dish and the red heart to the spoon handle.

19 Couch down embroidery floss around the outside edge of the spoon. Stab stitch around the red heart and the white dish. Couch down embroidery floss in a semi-circle to resemble the rim of the dish.

20 Work running stitch around the strawberries and green leaf shapes. Finally stitch tiny yellow seed beads at random on the strawberry shapes.

Birthday Cake
21 To make the cake, using the picture as a guide, position the plate on the background fabric and bond in place. Center the cake on the plate and the topping overlapping the cake side and bond in position. Position the candles on the cake. Tuck the flames under the tops of the candles and bond in position.

22 Couch a length of stranded embroidery floss around the plate shape. Work a running stitch around the inside of the pink topping and the candles. Stab stitch around the candle flame and the cake side.

23 Turn under ¼ in/0.6cm seam at each end of a 4¾ in/12.1cm length of ric rac braid. Couch the braid to the cake side. To finish, stitch multi-colored beads to the topping for decoration.

To Make the Book
NOTE: *If the fabric is thin and the designs show through the pages, place a lining fabric between the layers.*

24 To make up the book, trim the pages so that they are the same size. With right sides together and allowing ¼ in/0.6cm seam, baste, then stitch three sides of the girl and crown to page number one, leaving open the spine edge. Tidy the seams, turn right side out and press. Repeat this step stitching the gingerbread man to page number two, the mice to page number three, the balloons to page number four, the strawberries to page number five, and the cake with candles to the message page.

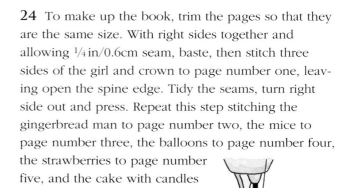

25 At the spine, turn under ⅝ in/1.6cm on all the pages, press and baste together. Machine topstitch close to the edge.

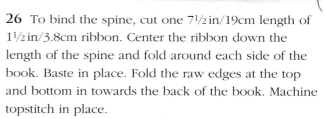

26 To bind the spine, cut one 7½ in/19cm length of 1½ in/3.8cm ribbon. Center the ribbon down the length of the spine and fold around each side of the book. Baste in place. Fold the raw edges at the top and bottom in towards the back of the book. Machine topstitch in place.

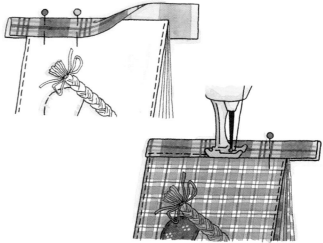

27 With the remaining ribbon, make a bow and stitch to the center of the spine binding.

CLOTH BOOK

Tail

59

For remaining Cloth book motifs see page 125

· TEDDY AND BUNNY QUILT ·

This warm and snuggly quilt has all-time favorite teddy and bunny appliqués. We used bright coordinated fabrics in primary colors but it would be great fun to use the furnishing fabrics from the child's own room for the borders or the animals' clothes.

Finished size 53 x 35in/134.6 x 88.9cm

MATERIALS

- ¼yd/0.25m of green check for the background fabric
- ¼yd/0.25m of blue check
- ¼yd/0.25m of green
- ¼yd/0.25m of blue
- ¼yd/0.25m of white for the bunnies
- ¼yd/0.25m of fawn for the teddies
- ¼yd/0.25m of light brown
- ¼yd/0.25m of dark brown
- ¼yd/0.25m of yellow stripe for the pieced blocks
- ¼yd/0.25m of yellow spot
- ¼yd/0.25m of plain yellow
- ¼yd/0.25m of yellow check
- Fabric scraps for the clothes
- ½yd/0.5m of 45in/114cm wide green and navy blue check for the border
- 5in/13cm of 45in/114cm wide yellow and green check for the border squares
- ½yd/0.5m of 45in/114cm wide plain yellow for binding
- 1yd/1m of 60in/152cm wide calico for backing
- 1yd/1m of 60in/152cm wide 4oz polyester batting
- 1¾yd/1.6m of fusible webbing
- 20 small brown buttons
- 20 small blue buttons
- 1 skein of yellow, green and blue coton à broder or pearl embroidery floss for tying the quilt

CUTTING OUT

1 To make the teddy and bunny appliqué motifs, trace the patterns provided to make your own templates.

2 Place the templates right side down on the paper side of the fusible webbing and mark an outline. Cut the required amount.

3 Place the template right side up on the fabric and mark an outline. Cut the required amount.

4 To make the background for the teddies and bunnies, cut five rectangles measuring 6 x 7½in/ 15.2 x 19cm in each of the blue, green, blue check, and green check fabrics.

5 To make the yellow blocks, cut one rectangle 19⅜ x 11⅝in/49.2 x 29.5cm from each shade. Fold the rectangle in half lengthwise, so that right sides are facing. Mark one line parallel with the foldline, 3⅞in/ 9.2cm from the top raw edge. At a right angle to the foldline, mark parallel lines 3⅞in/9.2cm apart. Pin the two sides together in each square. Cut along the marked lines. There will be 15 squares from each yellow shade.

6 To make the borders, cut twelve squares measuring 3½in/8.9cm square from the yellow and green check.

7 For the side borders, cut four strips measuring 10 x 3½in/25.4 x 8.9cm and four strips measuring 8¾ x 3½in/22.2 x 8.9cm in green and blue fabric.

8 For the top and bottom borders cut four strips

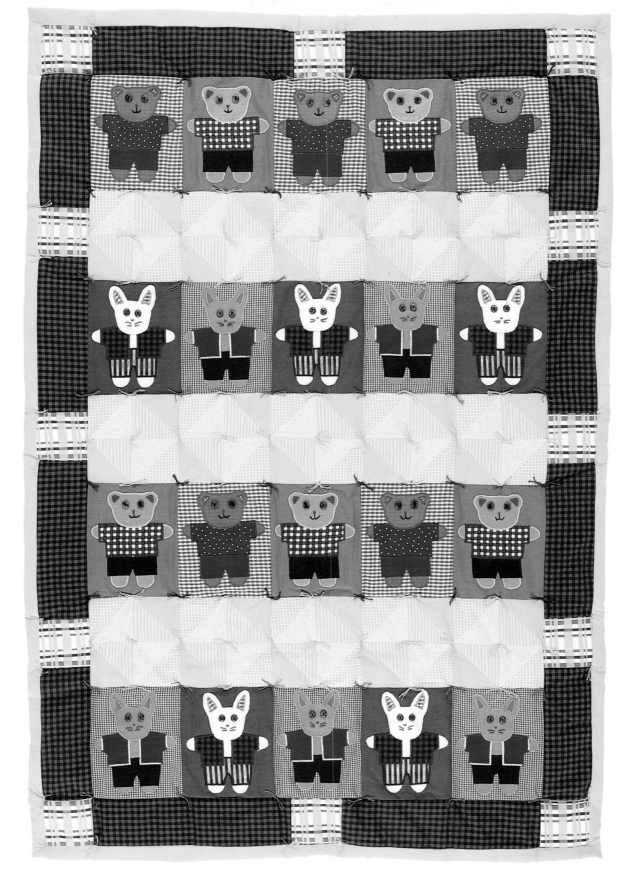

61

measuring 12 x 3½ in/30.5 x 8.9cm in the same green and blue check.

9 To make the binding, cut two strips 52 x 2½ in/ 132 x 6.4cm and two strips 36 x 2½ in/91.4 x 6.4cm.

MAKING UP

Use ¼ in/0.6cm seam allowance unless otherwise stated.

1 To make the teddy and bunny panels, iron fusible webbing to the wrong side of each fabric shape. Using the pattern as a guide, assemble each motif and place a piece of tearaway stabilizer at the back. Following the instructions on page 110 for bonding, iron each piece to the background fabric.

2 Using wide satin stitch, appliqué around the paws, shorts, tops, head and inside ear.

3 Stem stitch the features and stitch on buttons for eyes. Alternatively, embroider eyes or appliqué blue or brown circles.

4 With right sides together, stitch one bunny panel to one teddy panel to make four rows of five panels.

5 To make the yellow setting blocks, using two squares from different shades, place one on top of the other so that right sides are facing. With a fabric marker draw a diagonal line from corner to corner. Baste, then stitch a diagonal line at each side of the marked line, ¼ in/0.6cm from the center line.

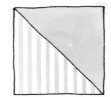 

Cut across the diagonal line to make two bi-colored squares. Repeat this step to make up a total of 60 bi-colored squares.

6 Arrange the squares into rows of ten, so that each triangle sits next to a different pattern. Baste, then stitch the squares together into six rows.

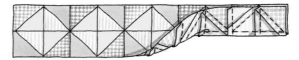

7 Stitch two rows of ten together. Repeat this for the remaining four rows.

8 With right sides together, stitch a yellow row to a teddy and bunny row. Repeat this step alternating the rows, until the four teddy and bunny rows and three yellow rows form one panel.

9 To make the side border, with right sides together, baste, then stitch one 10in/25.4cm long green and blue check rectangle to each side of a yellow and green check square. Stitch a square to each end of the border. Stitch one 8¾ in/22.3cm rectangle to each end. Finish by adding one square to each end. Trim the edges and press out the seams.

10 To make the top and bottom borders, with right sides facing, stitch one yellow and green check square to the center of two 12½ in/31.8cm long rectangles.

11 With right sides together, stitch the top and bottom borders to the quilt top. Trim the edges and press the seams open.

12 With right sides together, stitch the side borders to the main panel.

13 To make the quilt, lay the backing fabric right side down on a clean, flat, large surface. Place the batting on top, then the teddy and bunny panel right side up on top to make a quilt sandwich.

14 Baste the three layers together horizontally, vertically and diagonally and along each edge.

15 Tie the quilt top using coton à broder. To make a square knot, hold the needle and thread at the front of the quilt perpendicular to it. Stab through the three layers, leaving a length of thread behind long enough to tie a knot. Bring the needle back up through the quilt ⅛ in/0.3cm from the first stitch. Take the thread back down through the first stitch and up through the second. Pull tight. To make a square knot, work the ends of the thread, right over left, then left over right. Tie a knot at the corner of each teddy and bunny square, at the corner of each large yellow square and at the center of each yellow square.

16 Trim the backing fabric and batting to the same size as the front panel.

17 To attach the binding to the sides of the quilt, with right sides together, align the raw edge of the bias strip with the raw edge of the quilt, baste, then stitch in place. Trim the edges and press the seams out.

18 Repeat this step for the top and bottom, catching in the ends of the side binding.

19 Fold the binding back over the stitching line to the back of the quilt. Turn under ¼ in/0.6cm seam allowance on the raw edge of the binding and press in place. Slipstitch into place.

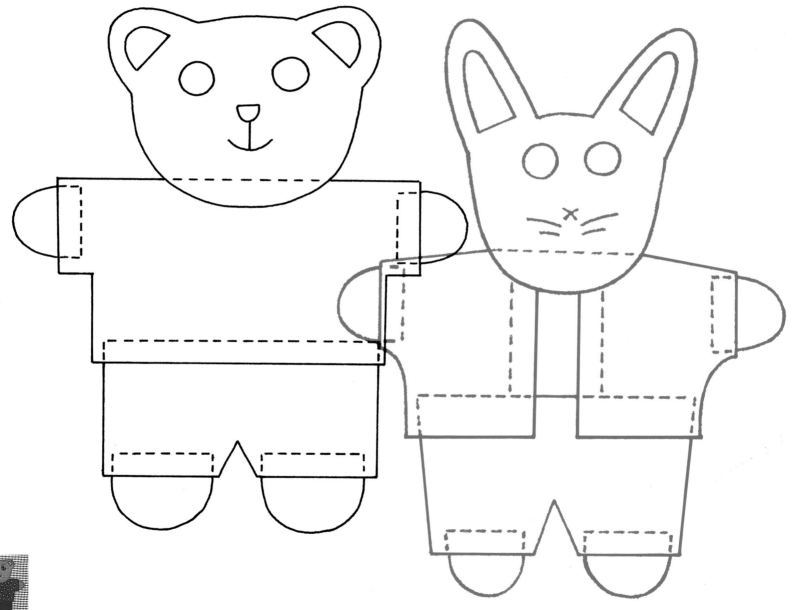

The
BATHROOM

· BATH MITTS ·

These brightly colored bath mitts are quick and easy to make
and will make bathtime a pleasure for any child.

*Finished size 4 ¹/₂ x 6 ¹/₂ in/11.4 x 16.5cm to fit a six
year old. Adapt the pattern for older children.*

MATERIALS
• Two different colored face cloths or equivalent
size pieces of terry cloth
• Fabric scraps for appliqué motifs
• 1yd/1m of jumbo cotton cord

CUTTING OUT
1 Trace the patterns provided for the mitt. Cut a front
and back from each face flannel.

2 Trace the appliqué motifs using the patterns
provided. Place the template right side up on the right
side of the fabric and trace an outline. Cut out each
shape, allowing a ¹/₄ in/0.6cm seam.

3 To cut the correct length of jumbo cotton cord,
measure the front mitt shape at the wrist, double the
measurement and add 5in/12.7cm.

MAKING UP
1 Turn under and press ¹/₄ in/0.6cm seam allowance
on all appliqué motifs.

2 Use the pattern to assemble and position the
lighthouse and puffin designs. Appliqué the motifs to
the front of each mitt using slipstitch. Work a tiny
running stitch across the top and bottom of each white
section on the lighthouse.

3 To sew the mitt together,
take one front and one back
in contrasting colors. Turn
under a ¹/₄ in/0.6cm seam
allowance and press. With
right sides together, baste,
then sew around the long
and curved edges of the
mitt, leaving the short,
straight wrist end open.
Tidy the raw edges. Turn
right side out.

4 At the wrist opening, turn under 1in/2.5cm of fabric, baste in place and secure with double topstitch.

5 Position the jumbo cord by aligning one end of the cord with a seam. Hand stitch in place around the fold of the wrist opening.

6 Make a loop with the excess cord and stitch the loose end into place by joining it to the starting point. Bind the raw edges of the cord to stop it unraveling. If you prefer, bind the wrist opening with bias binding or fabric.

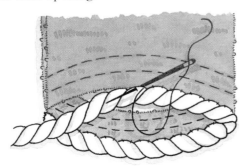

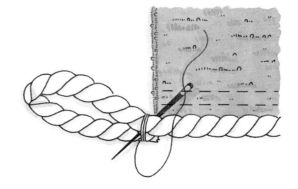

· STEAMER BAG ·

Bags of all shapes and sizes are popular with youngsters who just love stowing things away!
This super, roomy bag for bathroom paraphernalia is the perfect holiday companion especially if
traveling off and away over the sea!

Finished size 12 1/2 x 9 1/2 in/31.8 x 24.1cm

MATERIALS
- 1/2 yd/0.5m blue check fabric for the bag
- 1/2 yd/0.5m yellow lining
- 1/4 yd/0.25m fabric for the sea
- Scraps of royal blue, bright red, yellow, light blue, white, and red and navy check for the appliqué motifs
- 10in/25cm square of 2oz batting
- 12in/30.5cm zipper
- Two 1in/2.5cm D-rings
- 1yd/1m of No 6 piping cord
- 1/4 yd/0.25m fine cord for the zipper tag
- 1/2 yd/0.5m fusible webbing
- 1/2 yd/0.5m tearaway stabilizer
- 3 1/2 yd/3.2m of yellow bias binding to cover the seams on the inside of the bag

CUTTING OUT

1 For the bag, cut out one front and one back 10 1/2 x 13 1/4 in/26.7 x 33.7cm from the blue and white check fabric.

2 Cut one piece 34 x 4 1/2 in/86.4 x 11.4cm for the side-base-side gusset from the blue check fabric.

3 Cut two pieces 13 1/2 x 2 1/2 in/34.3 x 6.4cm for the bag top from the blue check fabric.

4 For the lining, cut out all the above pieces in yellow fabric. If preferred, the fabric could be substituted with a plastic lining if the bag is to be used as a swimming or beach bag.

5 For the appliqué motifs, trace the patterns provided to make templates. Place the templates right side up on the right side of the fabric and mark an outline. Cut out one set using the picture as a guide.

6 Place the appliqué templates right side down on the paper side of the fusible webbing and mark an outline. Cut out and iron the tacky side of the fusible webbing pieces to the wrong side of the fabric.

7 For the zipper tag, trace the template provided and cut out two circles of blue fabric 1/2 in/1.3cm larger than the template.

8 Cut two plastic circle—the tops of margarine cartons will do.

9 Cut two circles of 2oz batting the same size.

10 To make two tabs, cut two strips of fabric 1 3/4 x 1 1/2 in/4.5 x 3.8cm.

MAKING UP

1 Using the picture as a guide and following the instructions on page 110 for bonding, iron the sea fabric to the front blue check panel.

2 For the steamer, assemble the pieces before bonding them together. Position the pieces on the bag front. Build up the steamer by bonding the big pieces to the check fabric first.

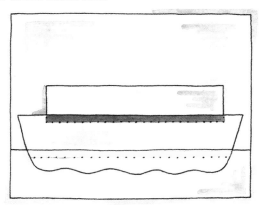

3 To make the flag, place wrong sides together, bond the back and front to each other. Stitch around the edges of the two long sides and one short side of the flag with a wide satin stitch. Trim away any loose threads. Bond the red flagpole over the unstitched edge of the flag. Ensuring that the flag flies freely, bond the flagpole to the steamer panel using the picture as a guide.

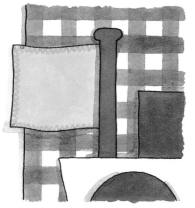

69

4 Following the manufacturer's instructions, place tearaway stabilizer behind the whole steamer motif to stop any puckering while stitching. Using wide satin stitch appliqué around each raw edge of the steamer.

5 Center the sea fabric on the side-base-side gusset and bond in position. Work a wide satin stitch around the raw edges on the side panels only.

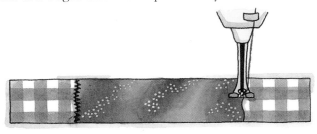

6 Using the picture as a guide, bond the sea fabric to the back panel of the bag. Work a wide satin stitch around the top raw edge of the sea.

7 Press all the panels on the wrong side.

8 For the zip panel, take one strip of blue check fabric and one strip of yellow lining fabric and place right sides together. Allowing ½ in/1.3cm seam, baste, then stitch two long edges and one short edge together. Tidy the seams and turn right side out. Turn under ½ in/1.3cm seam allowance at the opening and slipstitch together.

Repeat for the second strip.

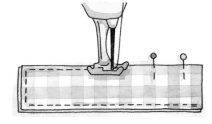

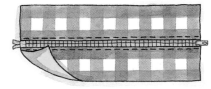

9 Insert the zip between them, following the instructions on page 71.

10 To make the tabs, fold the tab lengthwise. Press. Stitch one short end and the long end together. Turn right side out. Turn under ¼ in/0.6cm seam at the remaining short end and stitch together. Thread a tab through a ring and form a loop. Position a tab at each end of the gusset panel. Stitch on the wrong side of the fabric.

11 With wrong sides together, baste, then stitch the side and side lining together. Tidy the seams.

12 With right sides facing, align the two short edges of the side-base-side gusset with the short edges of the zipper panel. Allowing a ½ in/1.3cm seam, baste, then stitch together to form a circle.

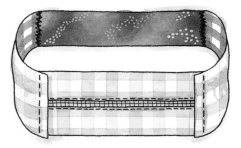

13 To attach the handles, cut two lengths of piping cord by gauging the length required. Position the cord on the wrong side of the back and front panels, 2½ in/6.5cm in from the side seam. Machine stitch on the seam line to secure.

14 Match each front and back lining panel to the corresponding front and back fabric panels. Allowing ½ in/1.3cm seam, with wrong sides facing, baste, then stitch together.

15 With right sides together, and using ½ in/1.3cm seam, ease the side panel onto the front panel. Baste, then machine stitch in place. Repeat this step for the back panel, making sure that you leave the zip open. Tidy all seam stitching. Check the seams are correctly sewn together and reinforce any stitching where appropriate.

16 To complete, bind all the seams with bias binding to match the color of the lining.

17 To make the zipper tag, bond the yellow anchor shape to the right side of one blue circle. Appliqué around the edges with satin stitch.

18 Hand stitch a gathering thread around each blue circle. With wrong side facing, overlay each blue disc with a piece of batting and a plastic disc. Pull up the gathering stitches to encase the disc inside. Adjust the gathers and lace the thread across the plastic disc to tighten and hold in place.

19 Attach a fine cord to the hole in the top of the zipper. Glue the cord to the plastic center of one circle, aligning it with the yellow anchor shape. Glue the two discs together so that the plastic discs and the cord are encased.

20 Ladder stitch the edges together. Slipstitch fine white cord around the outside to finish.

TO INSERT THE ZIP

1 Place the two long edges of the bag top side by side, right side up. Pin, then baste the pieces together with a zigzag stitch down the length of the center join.

2 On the lining side, center the zipper right side down over the join, vertically and horizontally. Mark the top and bottom of the zip on the lining. Remove the zipper. Stitch above and below the marked lines.

3 Replace the zipper over the center of the join. With a long straight stitch, baste down the length of the zipper at each side.

4 Machine stitch over the basting, taking care not to catch the teeth and ensuring that the fabric does not pucker. At the top and bottom, work a row of straight stitches. Reinforce top and bottom stitching.

5 Remove the straight and zigzag basting stitches.

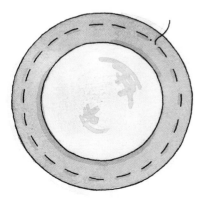

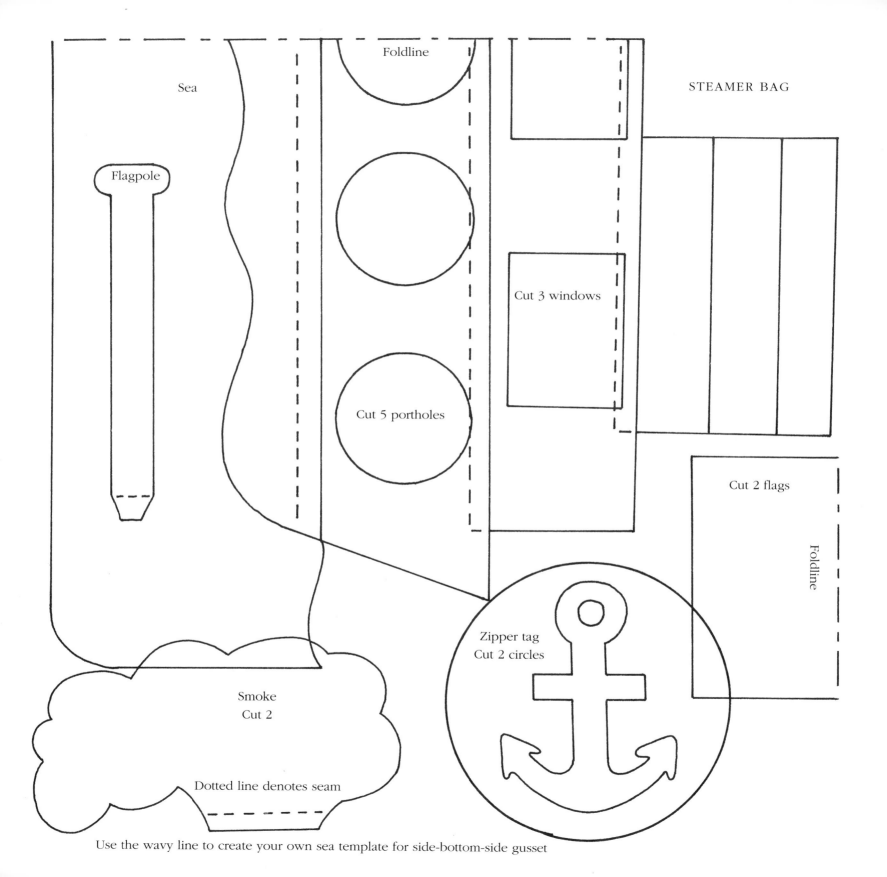

Sea

Foldline

STEAMER BAG

Flagpole

Cut 3 windows

Cut 5 portholes

Cut 2 flags

Foldline

Zipper tag
Cut 2 circles

Smoke
Cut 2

Dotted line denotes seam

Use the wavy line to create your own sea template for side-bottom-side gusset

· BATH ROBES ·

Equally at home in the bathroom, on the beach or at the pool, these stylish robes make a very personal statement for the wearer. Adapting a purchased bath robe takes away much hard work and leaves just the embellishment to tackle which can be great fun.

The pattern given is for a six year old, adapt the measurements and materials to fit older children.

MATERIALS
- A purchased terry cloth bath robe in an appropriate size
- 12in/30cm of 36in/90cm wide terry cloth for the belt and pockets in a contrast color
- Colorful cotton fabric scraps for the belt lining and appliqué motifs
- Small pieces of batting
- Ric rac braid for trimming
- Two decorative buttons for the fish pockets on the blue bath robe

CUTTING OUT

1 Measure the inside neck of your bath robe and add to it 1/2 in/1.3cm. Cut one strip of fabric the length of your measurement x 1 3/4 in/4.5cm wide.

2 For the loop to hang the bath robe, cut one strip of fabric 3 x 1in/7.6 x 2.5cm.

3 For the cuff, measure the circumference of the sleeve and add to this measurement 1/2 in/1.3cm. Cut two strips the length of your measurement x 3 1/2 in/ 8.9cm wide.

4 For the hem, measure the circumference of the bath robe hem and add 6in/15.3cm to your measurement. Cut one strip of fabric the length of the measurement x 3 1/2 in/8.9cm wide in fabric which matches the sleeve trim.

5 For the appliqué motif, trace the templates provided. Place the template right side up on the right side of the fabric, trace an outline and cut each shape.

6 For the fish pockets, enlarge the pattern for the slipper top by 135%. Cut two bodies and two fins. Use your fish template to cut two pieces of batting and lining the size of the fish.

7 For the belt, measure the length and width of the belt and cut one piece of terry cloth and one piece of fabric 1/2 in/1.3cm longer and wider.

MAKING UP

1 For the strip around the inside neck edge, turn under and press a 1/4 in/0.6cm seam allowance.

2 Place the fabric strip right side up over the inside neck seam, aligning the center of the strip with the center of the inside neck of the bath robe. Baste into place and machine topstitch to finish.

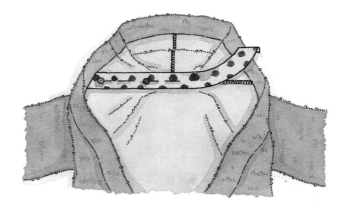

73

3 For the loop to hang the bath robe, turn under ¼ in/0.6cm seam all around. With wrong side facing, fold the strip in half down the length and press. Machine topstitch around the edge.

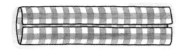

4 Position the strip horizontally, ¾ in/1.9cm below the neckline in the center back of the bath robe. Turn under the raw edges and pin in place. Stitch the short ends of the strip in place to form a loop. Reinforce the stitching.

5 For the cuffs, turn under and press a ¼ in/0.6cm seam allowance.

6 Work on each cuff separately. With right sides facing, fold the fabric across the width, holding the short ends together to form a circle. Baste, then sew across the short edge.

7 With right sides facing, slip the cuff over the sleeve. Baste, then stitch the bottom raw edge of the cuff 1½ in/3.8cm from the bottom of the sleeve. Tidy the edges.

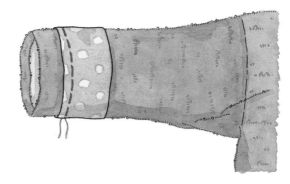

8 Turn the cuff back over the stitching line and press. Turn the remaining length of cuff inside the sleeve and press. Baste, then slipstitch in place.

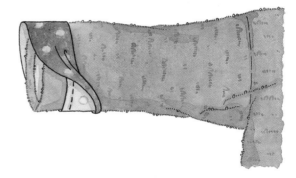

9 For the hem, turn under and press a ¼ in/0.6cm seam allowance.

10 With right sides together, place the center point of the fabric strip over the center point of the bottom of the bath robe, allowing the strip to extend beyond the

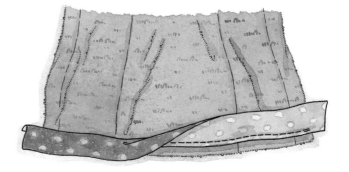

front edges. Position the fabric 1½ in/ 3.8cm above the bottom of the bath robe. Baste, then sew the bottom raw edge into place and tidy the seams. Turn the strip down over the stitching line and press. Turn the excess fabric inside the bath robe and press. Baste, then slipstitch in place.

11 Fold in the overlapping lengths at the front of the bath robe and press. Baste, then hand stitch to hold.

12 For the fish pockets, with right sides together, baste, then stitch the tail fins to the body and press. With the right side of the fish facing, place the lining

and then the batting on top. Baste, then sew the three layers together, leaving a small gap. Tidy the seams. Turn right side out and slipstitch across the opening.

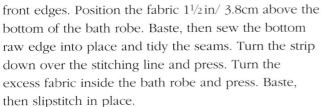

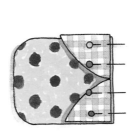

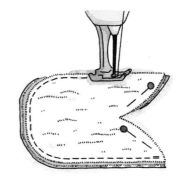

75

13 To finish, bind the fish fins with contrasting bias and stitch ric rac braid across the join.

14 Baste, then sew the pockets onto the bath robe and machine topstitch. Add a button for the eye and a tiny strip of bias for the mouth.

15 For the bath robe with the appliquéd puffin motif, turn under a ¼ in/0.6cm seam allowance on each piece of motif and press. Assemble the pieces using the template as a guide. Appliqué in place with slipstitch.

16 For the belt, turn under and press a ¼ in/0.6cm seam allowance on each of the terry cloth and fabric strips.

17 With wrong sides together, baste, then machine topstitch the fabric strip to the terry cloth.

· SLIPPERS ·

Super-easy slip-on slippers to match the fish pocket on the bath robe
will bring a smile to every child.

*The pattern given is for a six year old. Adapt the
pattern by measuring your child's foot.*

MATERIALS

- Canvas for the soles
- Two contrasting strong cotton fabrics for the tops
- Pieces of batting for the tops and soles
- Terry cloth for lining the tops and soles
- Contrasting bias binding

CUTTING OUT

1 Trace the pattern provided to make templates. Cut
out two fabric soles, two pieces of terry cloth lining
and two pieces of batting.

2 Cut contrasting fabric pieces for the slipper tops.
Cut out two pieces of terry cloth and batting.

MAKING UP

1 To make the soles, place the strong cotton fabric
right side down, cover with a piece of batting and
overlay with the terry cloth right side up. Baste the
three layers together and tidy the seams.

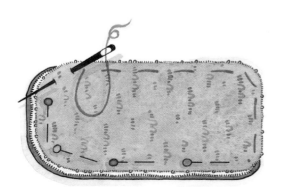

2 Starting halfway down the sole, working around the
heel and ending opposite your starting point, bind the
three layers together with bias binding. Overcast or
overlock the remainder of the sole.

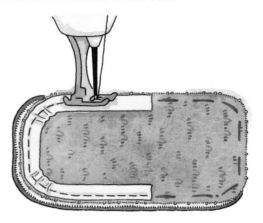

3 To make the slipper tops, with right sides together,
and allowing a ¼ in/0.6cm seam, baste, then sew the
slipper toe to the slipper fin. Press the seam down
towards the toe. Tidy the edges.

4 Place the terry cloth lining for the slipper top right side down, cover with batting, then place the top fabric right side up. Allowing a ¼ in/0.6cm seam, baste, then sew the three layers together. Tidy the seams. Overcast or overlock the edges.

5 Baste, then sew the bias binding along the top of the V shaped edge, keeping a neat edge at the center of the V. Repeat this step on the underside of the V shape.

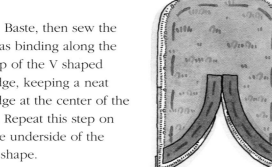

6 With fabric sides together and the terry cloth linings facing out, baste, then stitch the slipper top to the sole allowing a ¼ in/0.6cm seam. Tidy the edges.

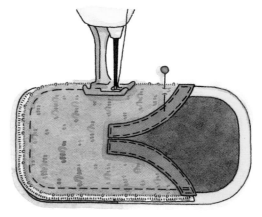

7 Strengthen the starting and finishing points with additional stitching.

8 Turn right sides out, and at the point where the bindings meet, hand stitch for extra strength.

78

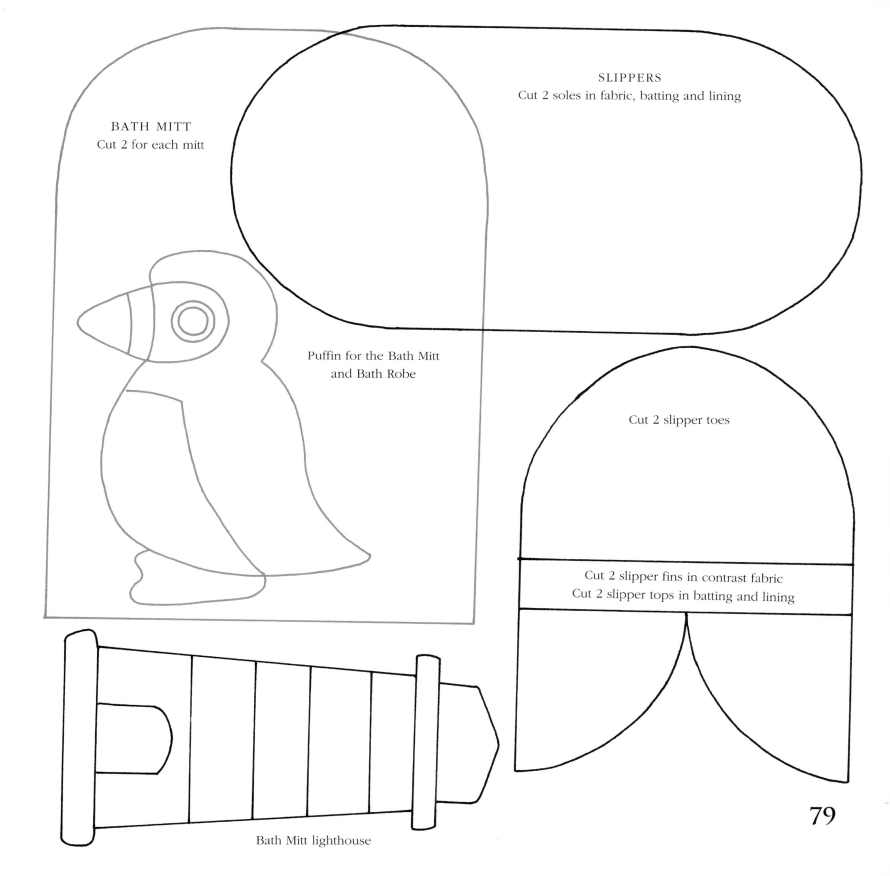

BATH MITT
Cut 2 for each mitt

SLIPPERS
Cut 2 soles in fabric, batting and lining

Puffin for the Bath Mitt
and Bath Robe

Cut 2 slipper toes

Cut 2 slipper fins in contrast fabric
Cut 2 slipper tops in batting and lining

Bath Mitt lighthouse

79

· HOODED TOWELS ·

Even the simplest everyday item can be personalized with a tiny appliqué motif. Choose any design from the book and reduce it to fit.

Finished size 29in/73.7cm square

MATERIALS
• A terry cloth in a suitable size or an equivalent length of terry cloth
• A large face cloth in a contrasting color
• One 16in/41cm strip of fabric cut on the straight to bind the diagonal edge of the hood
• 3yd 8in x 1¼in/3m x 3.2cm of continuous bias binding strip to bind the circumference of the towel
• Fabric scraps for appliqué motifs
• Small pieces of batting

CUTTING OUT

1 To prepare the terry cloth, cut off the manufactured finished edges and cut the terry cloth 29in/73.7cm square.

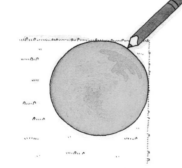

2 To make the corners round, draw a template from a small plate. Place the template on the towel in the corner, allowing it to touch two sides of the towel. Mark the outline of the plate on the terry cloth at the corner point and cut around the outline. Trim the remaining three corners to match.

3 To prepare the hooded corner, cut off the decorative edges of the face cloth and cut the cloth across the diagonal.

4 Trim one corner to match the corner of the hooded terry cloth and discard the remaining piece.

5 From the rounded corner of the face cloth to the diagonal, the hood should measure 6in/15.2cm. Mark this point and trim the diagonal length to match.

6 Measure the diagonal length of the hood and add 1in/2.5cm. Cut one strip of fabric this length x 2½in/6.4cm wide.

7 Measure the length of the circumference of the towel and cut a bias binding strip 1in/2.5cm longer x 1½in/3.8cm. Alternately, use a bias tape maker to make a bias binding and cut the strip according to the width required by the tape maker.

8 For the appliqué motifs, make a template by tracing the patterns provided. Place the template right side up on the right side of the fabric, trace the shape and cut out.

MAKING UP

1 For the hood, turn under and press a ¼in/0.6cm seam allowance along the long edges of the binding.

2 With wrong sides facing, fold the binding in half down the length and press.

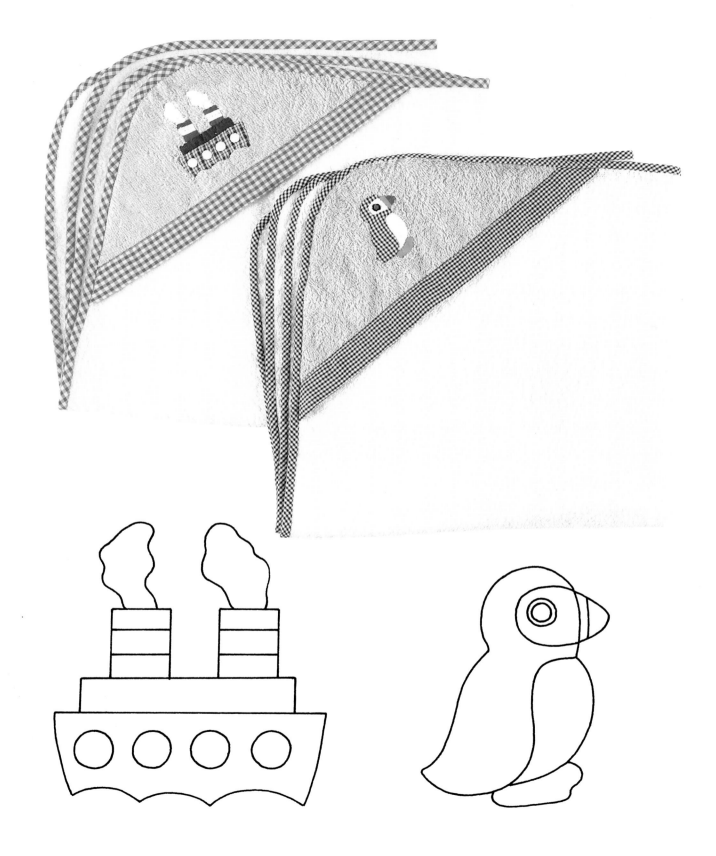

3 Slip the binding over the diagonal raw edge of the hood. Baste, then machine topstitch in place. Trim the short ends of the binding to shape along the sides of the face cloth.

4 Using the template as a guide, assemble the puffin pieces. Appliqué in place on the hood with slipstitch.

5 Alternately, using the template as a guide, assemble the boat pieces. Place a tiny piece of batting under the round white port holes before stitching to gain a textured effect. Appliqué in place with slipstitch. With a contrasting thread, hand stitch a line across the white portion of the funnel.

6 To attach the hood to the towel, with right sides up, align the rounded corners of the hood with the towel. Baste in place.

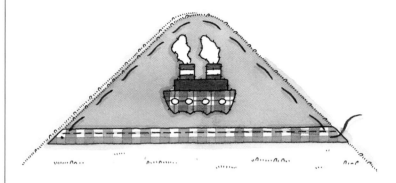

7 To attach the binding to the towel, turn under and press a ¼ in/0.6cm seam allowance on the long edges of the binding.

8 With wrong sides facing, fold the binding in half down the length and press.

9 Place the binding over the raw edges of the towel and hood, easing the binding around the corners. Baste, machine topstitch, then press to finish.

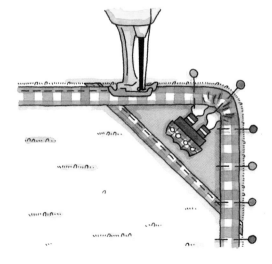

The
BEDROOM

· OWL QUILT ·

A whole family of owls keep guard through the night beneath the moon and the stars on this single-bed-sized quilt. A variety of checks and plaids give them a distinctive air and they will easily get names – McOwl, MacTwit, McTwhoooo...

Finished size 82 x 53½ in/208 x 135.9cm

MATERIALS

- 40in/1m of dark navy for the background of eight owl blocks
- 40in/1m of French blue for the background of eight owl blocks
- Fabric scraps for the owl bodies, wings and eyes
- 30in/76cm blue check fabric for the star background
- 30in/76cm of blue ground for the moon background
- 40in/1m yellow fabric for 20 gold stars, beaks and feet
- 30in/76cm yellow plaid fabric for 20 moons
- ½ yd/0.5m each of four different fabrics for sashing strips
- 2½ yd/3m of blue plaid fabric for the border
- 1yd 24in/1.5m of red check for the border
- 3yd/2.7m of 88in/223cm wide calico or sheeting for backing
- 2yd 10in x 1yd 18in/2.1m x 1.4m of 2oz batting for backing
- Fusible webbing for owls, moons and stars
- Embroidery floss

CUTTING OUT

1 For the 16 owl backgrounds, cut eight dark navy squares 9½ x 9½in/24.1 x 24.1cm.

2 Cut eight French blue squares 9½ x 9½in/ 24.1 x 24.1cm.

3 For the moon and star backgrounds, cut 20 blue check squares 6½ x 6½in/16.5 x 16.5cm.

4 Cut 20 night sky blue squares 6½ x 6½in/ 16.5 x 16.5cm for the moon background.

5 For the sashing cut 32 strips, 9½ x 2in/24.1 x 5cm, and 32 strips 12½ x 2in/31.7 x 5cm from each piece of fabric.

6 Cut two blue border strips 54 x 2¾ in/137.2 x 7cm.

7 Cut two blue plaid border strips measuring 83 x 2¾ in/210 x 7cm.

8 Cut two red check border strips measuring 49 x 1in/124.5 x 2.5cm.

9 Cut two red check border strips measuring 79 x 1in/ 200.1 x 2.5cm.

10 Using the pattern provided, trace the owl, the wings, beak, feet and eyes to make templates.

11 Place the templates right side up on the right side of the fabric and mark an outline. Cut 16 bodies and 32 wings.

12 Place the templates right side up on the right side of the fabric and cut 16 beaks and 32 feet in yellow fabric.

13 From fabric scraps cut 32 eyes.

14 Place the templates right side up on the paper side of the fusible webbing, mark an outline. Cut 16 owl

bodies, 32 wings, 32 feet, 16 beaks and 32 eyes. Cut fusible webbing for 20 moons and 20 stars.

MAKING UP

1 To make the owl blocks, following the instructions for bonding on page 110, iron fusible webbing to the reverse of the owl pieces. Position each owl in the center of a block and tuck the raw edges of the wings underneath the body. Bond the owls to the block.

2 Appliqué around the raw edges of the shapes with satin stitch.

3 Using the pattern as a guide, position the eyes, beaks and feet and appliqué them to the owls using satin stitch. Press each block.

4 To make the moon and star blocks, iron fusible webbing to the wrong side of the moon and star shapes. Position one of each shape in the center of every 6½in/16.5cm block and bond in place.

5 Appliqué around the moon and star shapes with satin stitch. Press each block.

6 To attach sashing strips to each owl block, with right sides together and allowing ¼in/0.6cm seam, baste, then stitch the top sashing to the block, then stitch the bottom sashing to the block. Tidy the seam edges and press the seams towards the raw edges of the block. With right sides together, baste, then stitch the left-hand sashing across the end of the bottom sashing, the block and the end of the top sashing. Repeat this step for the right-hand sashing. Tidy the seam edges and press towards the raw edges.

7 Trim each block to measure 12in/30.5cm square.

8 With right sides together, and using ¼in/0.6cm seam, baste, then stitch the owl blocks together in four rows of four blocks.

9 With right sides together and allowing ¼in/0.6cm seam, baste, then stitch alternate stars to alternate moon blocks using the photograph as a guide. Press the seams out.

10 Repeat this step until five rows of eight alternating blocks of moons and stars have been completed.

11 With right sides together and allowing ¼ in/0.6cm seam, baste, then stitch the bottom of a row of moon and star blocks to the top of a row of owl blocks. Repeat this step alternating the rows and ending with a moon and star row. Tidy all the edges and press the seams out from the center.

12 To attach the red check border, find the center of the red check border and match it to the center of the top panel. Using a ¼ in/0.6cm seam allowance, baste, then stitch one length to the top of the panels. Repeat for the bottom of the panels. Trim the edges. Repeat this step for the side panels and miter the four corners, following the instructions on page 111.

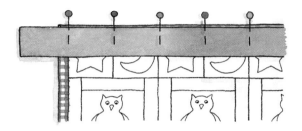

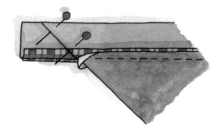

13 Repeat this step for the blue plaid borders. Turn under and press ¼ in/0.6cm seam allowance around the outside of the owl panel.

14 To stitch the owl panel to the batting and backing, spread the backing fabric out on a flat surface, right side down. Center the batting on top, then the quilt top right side up to make the quilt sandwich. The backing should be at least 1in/2.5cm larger than the owl panel and the batting.

15 Baste the three layers together horizontally, diagonally and vertically and along each edge.

16 Tie the quilt using red embroidery floss. Insert the needle at each front corner of the owl panel, make a stitch, then knot the thread tightly at the front. Trim the ends to ½ in/1.3cm long for decoration. Repeat this step at every corner. Use the picture as a guide.

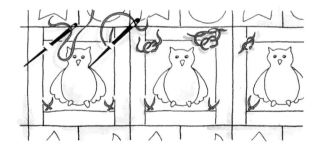

17 Fold the backing fabric over the batting to the inside of the quilt sandwich. Stitch the folded edges of the owl panel and the backing fabric together with an invisible slipstitch.

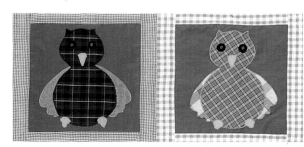

· OWLS ON A FENCE ·

These three jolly night owls are bound to become a bedtime favorite.

Finished size 25 x 13¾ in/63.5 x 34.9cm

MATERIALS

- A selection of shades of blue fabric strips at least 1yd/1m long for the sky
- A selection of green fabric scraps equivalent to ¼ yd/0.25m, to make 20 strips 6in/15cm long for the fence
- Fabric scraps for moon, stars, beaks, feet and wings
- Three different brown patterned fabrics for each owl body, measuring ¼ yd/0.25m square for the large bird and 7in/18cm square for the two smaller birds
- Three 5in/13cm circles for the owl breast
- One ¼ yd/0.25m square and two 7in/18cm squares of thin backing fabric such as lawn or butter muslin for each owl
- One ¼ yd/0.25m square and two 7in/18cm squares of batting for each owl
- Embroidery floss
- 26 x 19in/66 x 48cm of backing for the cushion
- 2¼ yd/2.05m of fine piping cord
- 3in/8cm of 45in/115cm wide blue fabric to make the cover for the piping cord
- A cushion pad measuring 25 x 13¾ in/63.5 x 34.9cm

CUTTING OUT

1 For the sky, cut ten lengths from a variety of blue fabric each 34 x 2in/86.3 x 5cm.

2 For the fence, cut 20 lengths each 5½ x 1¾ in/ 13.8 x 4.5cm.

3 For the owls, moon and stars, trace the patterns provided to make templates. The body and wing sections of each owl should include the tummy circle. Place each template right side up on the right side of the fabric scraps and mark an outline. Cut out each shape carefully on the pencil line.

4 Trace the outline of the owls, right side up on the batting and backing fabric. Cut out each shape.

5 To make the piping, cut the blue fabric in two along the length to form two strips.

6 To make the cushion back, cut two lengths of fabric 9¹/₂ x 26in/24.1 x 66cm.

MAKING UP

1 To make the sky, with right sides facing and allowing a ¹/₄ in/0.6cm seam, sew the ten 34in/ 86.3cm blue fabric lengths together. Tidy the seam edges and press out.

2 Measure and mark the pieced fabric every 2in/5cm across the vertical length and cut. Tidy the edges and press the pieced seams in the same direction.

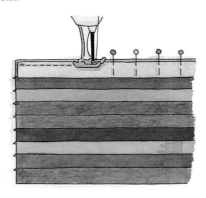

3 For the sky, make up a pieced rectangle measuring 25¹/₂ x 9¹/₂in/64.7 x 24.1cm from the pieced strips cut in step 2. Position the rows on a diagonal so that each block is placed next to a different color. With right sides together and allowing a ¹/₄ in/0.6cm seam, stitch the lengths together, ensuring all the joins are matched.

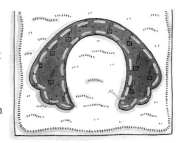

4 To make the fence, with right sides together and allowing ¹/₄ in/0.6cm seam, sew all the strips together lengthwise, alternating plain and patterned fabrics. Tidy the edges and press.

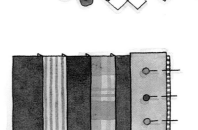

5 Using ¹/₄ in/0.6cm seam allowance and with right sides together, sew the sky to the fence. Trim the edges of the sky and press the seams.

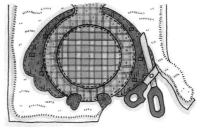

6 To make the owls, layer the backing fabric, batting and the wing right side up. Allowing a ¹/₈ in/0.3cm seam, baste the three layers together, then stitch around the outline.

7 Using the pattern as a guide, position the body on top of the wings, and stitch around the outline. Repeat this step, placing the tummy circle, beak and feet in position on top of the body. Without breaching the stitching line trim the backing fabric.

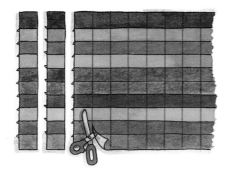

8 Appliqué with medium satin stitch around all the internal shapes only, ensuring that the raw edges are enclosed.

9 Using the picture as a guide, position the owls on the background with their feet overlapping the fence. Baste, then stitch the owl shapes to the background fabric.

10 Using wide satin stitch, appliqué the owls to the background to cover the raw edges.

11 Position the moon and stars using the picture as a guide. Baste, then appliqué into place, using satin stitch.

12 To make the cushion back, turn under ¼ in/ 0.6cm seam along one long edge and press. Turn under 1½ in/3.8cm on the same edge and press. Machine topstitch the hem ¼ in/0.6cm from the edge and again 1¼ in/3.2cm from the edge.

13 To make an envelope backing, with right sides face down, lay out the two lengths on a flat surface. Overlap one hem over the other by 1¾ in/3.8cm until the width of the cushion measures 14¼ in/36.2cm. Baste, then stitch the two layers together where they meet in the center.

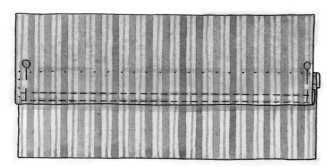

14 To make the piping cord, cut one end of each strip across the grain at a diagonal.

Allowing ¼ in/0.6cm seam, stitch the two diagonal edges together. Press the seam out.

15 Center the length of piping cord on the wrong side of the binding. Fold one edge of the binding over the cord to make a sandwich and baste the two layers of binding together close to the cord. Position the piping cord around the edge of the right side of the front panel, with the raw edges facing out and the piping cord facing the center of the cushion. Without catching the piping cord, clip the raw edges around the corners to make the piping flexible.

16 With right sides together, position the backing fabric over the cushion front and the piping cord and baste the layers together. Using the zipper foot on the sewing machine, stitch the three layers together as close as possible to the piping cord, easing the cord around the corners. Trim the seams to tidy and press carefully.

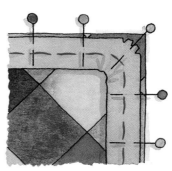

17 To complete the cushion, turn right side out and insert the cushion pad.

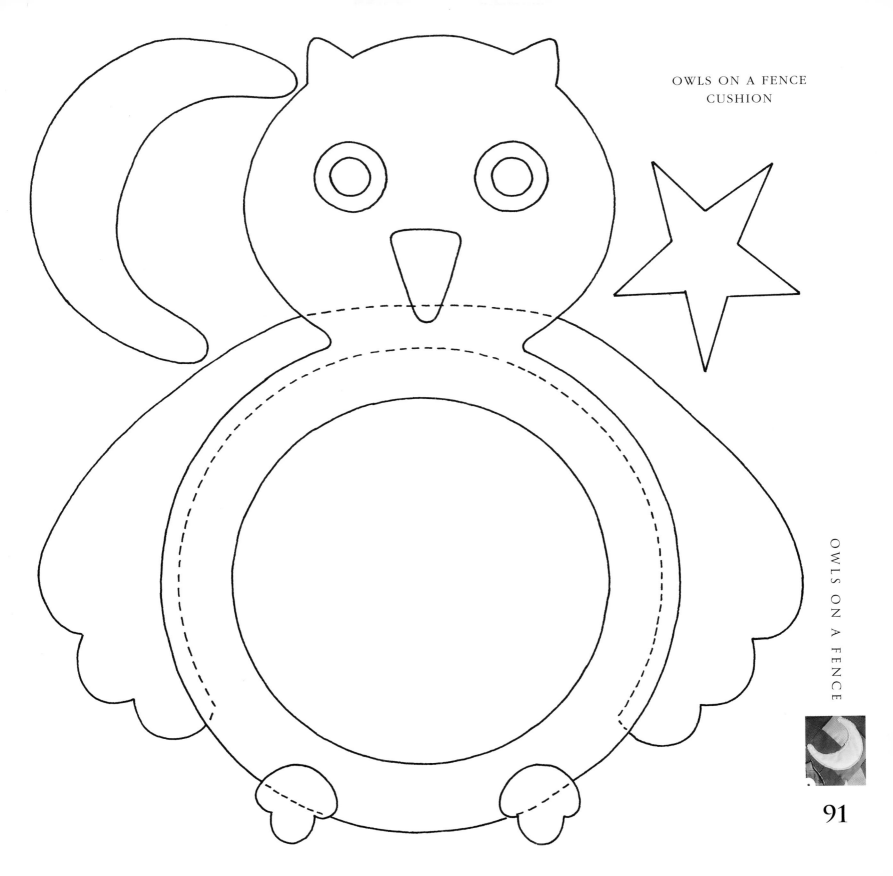

91

· CAT WALLHANGING ·

A soft, cuddly, contented cat sleepily sitting in a field of daisies. The trimmings add color and definition and the moon and stars dangle delightfully for eye-catching movement.

Finished size 12½ x 9½ in/31.8 x 24.1cm

MATERIALS

- 5 x 12in/13 x 30cm blue and white gingham for the background
- 11 x 12in/28 x 30cm of bright green cotton for the striped background, the border panels and folded triangles
- 13 x 9in/33 x 23cm medium blue cotton for the background panel, corner posts, backing and back pocket
- 10in/25cm square of red and tan plaid cotton for the cat
- 10 x 12in/25 x 30cm yellow cotton for the borders and hanging stars
- ¼ yd/0.25m square red and gold check cotton for the outer border, binding and hanging moon
- Fabric scraps for the white dots in the foreground, spotted yellow stars and red star centers
- 10in/25cm square fusible fleece for backing the cat
- 10 x 13in/25 x 33cm pelmet weight Pellon or buckram
- 8 x 9in/20 x 23cm light weight canvas, calico or stiff Pellon fusible interfacing for interlining the moon and stars
- ½ yd/0.5m fusible webbing
- 38in/97cm narrow, light blue ric rac braid
- 14in/36cm medium, red ric rac braid
- 3in/8cm narrow, red ric rac braid
- 14in/36cm royal blue ric rac braid
- Embroidery floss
- 12 x 9in/30 x 23cm of light cardboard for stability—use a cereal packet
- 10in/25cm red cord for hanging

CUTTING OUT

1 For the striped background, cut twelve strips of blue and white gingham ⅞ x 4½ in/2.2 x 11.4cm and eleven strips of bright green 1 x 4in/2.5 x 10.2cm.

2 For the side borders, cut two strips of bright green 1½ x 7½ in/3.8 x 19.1cm.

3 For the folded triangles at the base, cut five 2½ in/6.4cm squares from the green fabric. Cut five 1in/2.5cm squares from light cardboard.

4 For the back pocket, cut one piece of medium blue cotton 10½ x 12½ in/26.7 x 31.8cm.

5 For the backing fabric, cut one piece of medium blue 9¾ x 12½ in/24.8 x 31.8cm.

6 For the background panel, cut one piece of medium blue 3¾ x 9¾ in/9.5cm x 24.8cm.

7 For the corner blocks, cut four squares in medium blue 1½ in/3.8cm.

8 For the borders, cut two strips of yellow 1½ x 9¾ in/3.8 x 24.8cm.

9 For the binding, cut two strips of red and gold check fabric 1½ x 13in/3.8 x 33cm and two strips 1½ x 10in/3.8 x 25.4cm.

10 For the cat appliqué motif, trace around the outer line of the pattern provided to make a template. Placing the template right side up on the bias grain of

93

the right side of the fabric, mark the outline and cut one shape in red and tan plaid.

11 Cut the ¼in/0.6cm seam allowance from the cat template. Place the template, right side up on the fusible fleece with the sticky side up and trace the outline. Cut one shape.

12 For the stars, trace the template provided. Place the template on the fabric and cut out eight shapes, four from the yellow fabric and four from the spotted yellow fabric.

13 Using the same templates, cut four pieces of fusible interfacing for interlining.

14 For the moon, trace the template provided. Place on the right side of the fabric and mark an outline. Cut out two shapes from the red and gold check.

15 Using the template provided, cut out one piece of fusible interfacing for interlining.

16 From the narrow, light blue ric rac braid, cut four strips 4in/10.2cm, one strip 2¾in/7cm, one strip 2in/5.1cm, two strips 1¾in/4.5cm, two strips 1¼in/ 3.1cm, and one strip 1in/2.5cm.

17 For the white polka dots, iron fusible webbing to the wrong side of the white fabric scrap. Cut out 16 ½in/1.3cm circles.

18 For the hanging cord, cut two lengths of red cord 5in/12.7cm.

MAKING UP

1 For the vertical stripes behind the cat, stitch the ric rac braid down the center of the green fabric in the following sequence: 4in/10.2cm three times; 2in/5cm six times; and 4in/10.2cm twice. The cat motif will cover the shorter ends of the ric rac braid.

2 Allowing a ¼in/0.6cm seam and with right sides together, stitch alternate strips of blue and white gingham and bright green together. Start and finish with gingham and ensure that the green strips are sewn in the correct sequence.

3 Tidy the edges and press the seams towards the green strips.

4 Press the whole panel. Tidy the bottom edge of the panel to form a rectangle 9¾ x 4in/24.8 x 10.2cm.

5 For the blue polka dot panel, use the picture as a guide to position the white circles on the blue background fabric. Following the instructions for bonding on page 110, bond the circles in place.

6 With four strands of blue embroidery floss, stitch around each spot with blanket stitch.

7 With right sides together, baste, then stitch the top of the polka dot panel to the bottom of the striped panel. Press the seam towards the blue panel and tidy the edges. Trim the bottom of the panel to form a rectangle 7½ x 9¾in/19.2 x 24.8cm. Put the panel to one side.

8 For the cat, use the template as a guide to mark the eyes, whiskers, mouth, paw and leg lines with a fine pencil.

9 For the inner ear, make a template from the pattern provided. Place the template right side up on the paper side of the fusible webbing and mark an outline. Cut out the shapes and iron onto the russet fabric. Following the instructions for bonding on page 110, bond the ears to the face, using the template as a guide. Machine appliqué around the shapes with narrow satin stitch.

10 Make a nose in the same manner using unbleached calico or fabric scraps and apply in the same way.

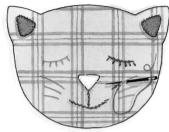

11 Using three strands of floss, embroider the whiskers, mouth and eyes in stem stitch.

12 Fuse the fleece to the wrong side of the body and head allowing a ¼ in/0.6cm seam. Turn under and press the seam allowance around the fleece except for the neck edge on the body piece.

13 Place the cat motif fleece side down on the fabric panel, ensuring that the ends of the ric rac braid are covered and that the neck is tucked under the head. Baste in place.

14 Appliqué the motif to the background using slipstitch.

15 Stem stitch around the entire cat using three strands of embroidery floss. Embroider the paw and leg lines to complete.

16 To make the borders, stitch the red ric rac braid to the center of each yellow border strip.

17 Embroider a large running stitch ³/₈ in/1cm from each edge using five strands of embroidery floss.

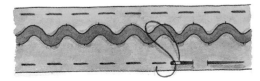

18 Stitch the blue ric rac braid to the center of the green border strips. Trim the borders to match the side of the rectangular cat panel.

19 With right sides together and allowing a ¼ in/ 0.6cm seam, baste, then stitch a blue corner block to each end of the green borders. Tidy the edges and press the seam allowance towards the blue corner.

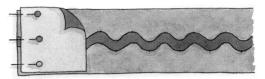

20 With right sides together and allowing a ¼ in/ 0.6cm seam, baste, then stitch the yellow borders to the top and bottom of the cat panel. Tidy the edges and press the seam allowance towards the yellow border. Trim the borders to the same size as the panel.

21 With right sides together and allowing ¼ in/0.6cm seam, baste, then stitch the green borders and blue corner blocks to the side of the cat panel. Tidy the edges and press the seam allowance towards the green border.

22 To make the pocket, turn under a ¼in/0.6cm seam allowance on the medium blue fabric measuring 12½ x 10½in/31.8 x 26.7cm. Along one long edge turn under a second ¼ in/0.6cm seam allowance, and then a further ³/₄ in/1.9cm to make the hem. Baste, then stitch in place and press.

23 To make the backing panel, position the wrong side of the pocket with the hem at the top, ⁵/₈ in/1.6cm below the top of the backing fabric, right side up.

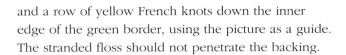

24 Place the backing fabric and pocket right side down and cover with pelmet weight Pellon. Allowing ¼ in/0.6cm seam, baste, then stitch the layers together. Stitch a second line ¾ in/1.9cm from the outside edge, using a long straight stitch.

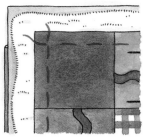

25 With right sides up, place the cat panel on the Pellon backing, allowing a ⅜ in/1cm seam and baste.

26 To bind the outer border, with wrong sides facing, fold the red and gold plaid fabric strips in half along the length and press. Turn under the two raw edges to the center and press again.

27 With right sides together, place the raw edge of one short length of binding over the raw edge of one side of the panel with the crease towards the center of the motif. Baste, then stitch in place.

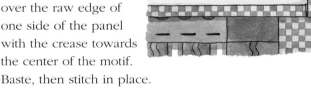

28 Turn the binding over to the back, press, then slipstitch in place, covering the line of machine stitching. Repeat this step for the second side. Trim the ends.

29 Turn under ¼ in/0.6cm seam allowance at each end of the binding fabric. With right sides together and allowing ¼ in/0.6cm seam, stitch one length of red and gold plaid to the top of the panel, catching in the top of the binding on the side panel. Turn the binding over to the back of the wallhanging and slipstitch in place. Repeat this step for the bottom of the panel.

30 To complete the borders, make a row of red French knots down the outer edge of the green border and a row of yellow French knots down the inner edge of the green border, using the picture as a guide. The stranded floss should not penetrate the backing.

31 To make the hanging stars and moon, bond fabric pieces to each side of the interlining using fusible webbing. If you are using iron-on Pellon interfacing, bond this to one piece of fabric and then bond the other piece of fabric to the interfacing.

32 With pinking shears cut two circles from bright red fabric and bond to the center of the two plain yellow stars. Blanket stitch around the outside edges of the moon and stars.

33 Cut three pieces of narrow blue ric rac and lightly glue one end to the top of two stars and the moon. Cut two pieces of narrow red ric rac and lightly glue one end to the two remaining stars.

34 To make the green triangles, fold each square of green fabric in half to make a rectangle. Turn the two corners on the foldline in towards the center line to make a triangle. Tuck a piece of cardboard into each triangle and stitch to hold. Overcast the raw edges.

35 Arrange the triangles evenly on the back of the panel at the bottom and without penetrating the motif on the front, slipstitch in place.

36 Slip the other end of each ric rac braid attached to the moon and stars into the fold of the green triangle and stitch together.

37 To make the hanging cord, turn under ½ in/1.3cm at each end and stitch to the back of the wallhanging.

38 Measure the size of the pocket and cut some cardboard slightly smaller. Slide the cardboard into the pocket and secure with stitching.

Cut 2 for each moon

Place arrow on grain line

Clip into seam allowance to ease turning
Inner line denotes seam

Cut 2 for each star

Polka dot

Star center

· SLEEPY BEAR PYJAMA CASE ·

Anything that encourages the tinies to be tidy is good training and a help to mom!

Finished size 14³/₄ x 14in/37.5 x 35.6cm when closed

MATERIALS

- ½ yd/0.5m of blue stripe cotton fabric for the bag
- ¼ yd/0.25m of cream cotton for the bear's pillow
- 5in/13cm of green check for the bear's sheet
- ½ yd/0.5m lining
- ¼ yd/0.25m of red fabric for binding
- Fabric scraps for the appliqué motifs
- 1yd x 14in/1m x 36cm of 2oz batting
- Embroidery floss
- Small ball of blue and white wool for the pom-pom
- Two large decorative buttons
- ¼ yd/0.25m square of fusible webbing
- 14 x 12in/36 x 30cm of tearaway stabilizer
- Small amount of Velcro to fasten

CUTTING OUT

1 Cut one length of cream fabric measuring 8½ x 11½ in/21.6 x 29.2cm.

2 Cut the green check fabric to measure 3½ x 11½ in/8.9 x 29.2cm.

3 Cut one length of blue stripe fabric to measure 2 x 11½ in/5 x 29.2cm.

4 Cut two lengths of blue stripe fabric 2 x 13in/ 5 x 33cm.

5 Cut one piece of blue stripe fabric for the back 17 x 14in/43.2 x 35.6cm.

6 For the lining, cut one front, 15 x 14in/

38.1 x 35.6cm and one back 17 x 14in/43.2 x 35.6cm. Cut the same in batting.

7 Cut two lengths of red fabric for the binding 1½ in x 2½ yds/3.8cm x 2.29m.

8 Trace the patterns provided to make templates for the bear appliqué motifs. Place the templates right side up on the right side of the fabric and trace an outline. Cut out each shape.

9 Place the templates face down on the paper side of the fusible webbing and trace an outline. Cut out the shapes leaving a narrow seam allowance around the edges.

10 Bond the pieces to the fabric shapes with a hot iron.

MAKING UP

1 To make the bear panel, with right sides together, baste, then stitch the cream and green check fabrics together along the length. Press the seam open.

2 Peel the paper from the back of the bear shapes and using the picture as a guide, assemble the bear pieces. Place the wrist of the bear's paw just under the the wrist of the nightshirt sleeve and the nightshirt neck edge just under the face. Place the inner ear under the hat. Position the pointed hat piece last. Following the instructions on page 110, bond the pieces in position.

3 Place tearaway stabilizer under the cream and green background panel. With a wide satin stitch appliqué around all the raw edges of the bear shapes.

4 Using three strands of embroidery floss, stem stitch and long stitch the features on the bear.

99

5 To make the pom-pom, trace the template provided onto cardboard and cut two. Place the circles on top of each other. Wind the white and blue wool around the circles until the hole in the center of the cardboard is filled in with wool.

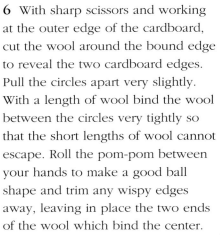

6 With sharp scissors and working at the outer edge of the cardboard, cut the wool around the bound edge to reveal the two cardboard edges. Pull the circles apart very slightly. With a length of wool bind the wool between the circles very tightly so that the short lengths of wool cannot escape. Roll the pom-pom between your hands to make a good ball shape and trim any wispy edges away, leaving in place the two ends of the wool which bind the center.

7 Sew the pom-pom onto the night cap with the wool ends and fasten securely.

8 To make the bag, place right sides together. Allowing a ¼ in/0.6cm seam, baste, then stitch the bottom of the green front bear panel to a 2 x 11½ in/ 5 x 29.3cm blue stripe length. Tidy the edges and press the seam open.

9 With right sides together and allowing ¼ in/0.6cm seam, baste, then stitch the side borders to the bear panel. Tidy the edges and press the seams open.

10 Measure the bear panel and cut the batting and lining ½ in/1.3cm larger all around.

11 With the panel right side down, center the batting and then the lining fabric on top. Baste the three layers together.

12 Using coton à broder, work a quilting stitch down both sides of the bear panel ¼ in/0.6cm inside the raw edge. Trim away the excess batting and lining to the same size as the front panel.

13 Place the blue stripe fabric for the back of the bag face down. Cover with a piece of batting and a piece of lining cut to the same size. Baste around the outside edges.

14 To stitch the binding to the panel, with wrong side facing, fold a strip of red binding fabric in half along the length. Press in place. Turn under the raw edges ¼ in/0.6cm towards the center foldline and press in place. Slide the binding over the edges of the panel and machine topstitch in place.

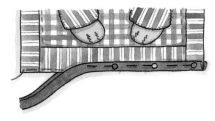

15 With wrong sides together, lay the bear panel on top of the back, aligning the bottom edges. Baste, then bind the bottom edge. Finish off securely. Bind the top edge of the back panel and the two sides, turning in the binding at the ends and finishing off securely.

16 Stitch two large, decorative buttons onto the flap at each side. For easy use, for young children stitch Velcro tabs to the inside flap to fasten.

Fold

Fold

Pom-pom
Cut 2

Fold

Dotted line denotes seam

101

· PIG AND RABBIT BAGS ·

A simple envelope-style bag with a big, bold appliqué design on the front which is fun to make and fun to use. Just the bag to help mom with the shopping!

Finished size 7¼ x 8½ in/18.4 x 21.6cm

MATERIALS FOR PIG BAG

- 17 x 8in/43 x 20cm of blue and white stripe cotton for the bag
- 6in/15cm square of spotted pink cotton for the pig
- 7 x 4in/18 x 10cm of yellow fabric for the panel
- 10in/25cm square of red and white gingham for the binding and handles
- Scraps of unbleached calico or muslin for the snout and inner ears
- Fabric scraps for the apple, leaf, stem, and trotters in appropriate colors
- 17 x 8in/43 x 20cm of heavy calico for lining
- 10 x 5in/25 x 13cm of medium weight iron-on Pellon interfacing
- ½yd/0.5m of fusible webbing
- Two flat green buttons for the eyes, ½in/1.3cm
- Two flat pink buttons for the snout, ⅜in/0.9cm

MATERIALS FOR RABBIT BAG

- 17 x 8in/43 x 20cm of blue spotted cotton for the bag
- 8 x 6in/20 x 15cm of spotted tan fabric for the rabbit shape
- 10 x 4in/25 x 10cm of green check fabric for the panel, binding and handles
- Fabric scraps for the carrot, inner ears, leaf-top
- ½yd/0.5m of fusible webbing
- 17 x 8in/43 x 20cm of heavy calico for lining
- 10 x 5in/25 x 13cm of medium weight fusible Pellon
- Embroidery floss
- Two flat blue buttons for the eyes, ½in/1.3cm in diameter

CUTTING OUT

1 For the appliqué motifs, using the patterns provided, trace the shapes to make templates. Place the templates right side up on the right side of the fabric scraps and mark an outline. Cut out each shape.

2 Following the pattern provided mark with pencil the whiskers and mouth on the rabbit. Using three strands of embroidery floss, stem stitch the mouth and whiskers of the rabbit.

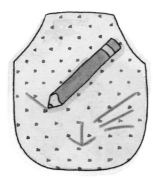 

3 Place the templates paper side down on the fusible webbing and mark each shape. With the exception of the pig's snout, iron the fusible webbing to the wrong side of the fabric shapes, but do not remove the paper at this stage.

4 For the handles, cut two strips of the appropriate colors 9¼ x 2½in/23.5 x 6.4cm.

5 For the binding cut two strips of the appropriate colors 7¾ x 2½in/19.7 x 6.4cm.

6 For the bag, iron the fusible webbing to the wrong side of the blue and white stripe fabric for the pig; and blue spotted fabric for the rabbit bag. Remove the paper and bond to the wrong side of the lining fabric.

7 Cut out a panel from the spotted yellow fabric for the Pig Bag, or green check fabric for the Rabbit Bag measuring 6 x 2³⁄₄ in/15.2 x 7cm. Cut a panel the same size from fusible webbing. Iron the fusible webbing to the wrong side of the fabric panel.

MAKING UP

1 Position the panel on the bag front 5in/12.7cm from one short edge and equal distance from each side. Peel off the paper backing from the fusible webbing panel and pin in place, but do not bond together.

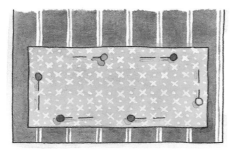

2 Using the photograph as a guide, assemble the pig or rabbit appliqué motifs and position on the bag front. Place the body seam allowance under the panel and following the instructions for bonding on page 110, fuse the panel but not the body to the background fabric.

3 Appliqué around the edge of the panel with satin stitch, sewing over the pig or rabbit body but leaving gaps for the trotters or paws.

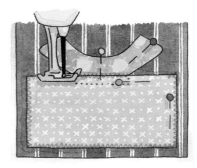

4 For the Pig Bag, pin the trotters in place, tucking the seam allowance under the body.

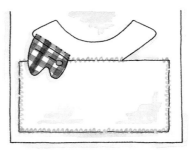

5 For both bags, fuse the body and trotters in place. Following the direction of the arrows on the template and using wide satin stitch, appliqué around the body outline, avoiding the area where the head joins the body. Appliqué across the join where the trotter meets the pig body.

6 Position the inner ears and bond to the background fabric. Appliqué in place using wide satin stitch.

7 Turn under ¹⁄₄ in/0.6cm seam allowance around the snout. Press and baste into place on the head. Slipstitch in place.

8 Bond the head in place on the body and appliqué around the outline using wide satin stitch, avoiding the area where the rabbit's ear joins the head.

9 For the Rabbit Bag, position the ear on the head and appliqué in place using a narrow satin stitch.

10 For the Pig Bag, position the apple on the yellow panel using the picture as a guide. Appliqué around the outline. Repeat this step for the stalk and the leaf.

11 Stitch the buttons for the eyes and snout into position.

12 Trim the bag to measure 17 x 8in/43.2 x 20.3cm.

13 Machine overcast the raw edges of the bag shape.

14 For the binding, machine overcast one long edge on two binding strips.

15 With right sides together, place the raw edge of the binding strip along the raw edge of the bag. Baste, then stitch allowing a $5/8$ in/1.6cm seam.

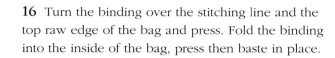

16 Turn the binding over the stitching line and the top raw edge of the bag and press. Fold the binding into the inside of the bag, press then baste in place.

17 Repeat this step for the second strip.

18 For the handles, fuse strips of Pellon measuring $9^{1}/_{4}$ x $1^{1}/_{4}$in/23.5 x 3.1cm to the center of the wrong side of the gingham fabric.

19 Fold the handle strips in half along the length and press carefully. Turn under the raw edges to the center of the strips, press and baste. Machine topstitch and edge stitch to finish the handles.

20 To secure the handles, pin the strips at the top

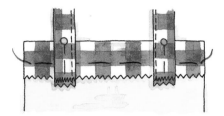

edge of the bag $1^{5}/_{8}$ in/4.1cm from the outside edges and with the bottom of the handles level with the bottom of the binding.

21 On the right side of the bag, machine topstitch the binding in place, then stitch across the base of the handles. Repeat on the other side, stitching across the base of the handles.

22 With right sides facing, fold the bag in half. Allowing a $3/8$ in/0.9cm seam, baste, then stitch the two long edges together. Stitch again $1/4$ in/0.6cm from the edge and tidy the seams.

23 Overcast the raw edges before pressing the seams out. For extra strength bind the inside seams. Turn the bag right side out and press.

105

· TECHNIQUES ·

ESSENTIAL EQUIPMENT

Tape Measure

Thimble

Pins
Use fine, stainless steel dressmaker's pins. For quilting, the long, glass-headed pins are best, and easy to identify in the bulk of the fabric. Discard burred or rusted pins as these will mark your fabric.

Needles
Machine needles are now universally sized and should fit most sewing machines. When using fine or medium weight cotton, a size 12 needle should be used, a heavier weight cotton will need a size 14. For quilting through polyester batting, a size 14 Teflon needle is ideal.

For hand stitching, packets of sharps, or hand embroidery needles containing a selection of needle lengths and sizes are readily available in shops. For fine, detailed work using two or three strands of embroidery floss, choose a needle with a small eye. Remember that some of the projects require beads, so the eye of the needle has to fit through the hole of the bead. For basting, use a long milliner's needle which can hold many stitches at one time.

Thread
As well as basting thread, you will need cotton thread for machine and hand stitching. If you are using 100% cotton fabrics, pick a good quality 100% cotton thread. Select a color that is a slightly darker shade than the fabric you are working with. If you are sewing many different colored fabrics, choose a neutral thread that will blend with all of your fabrics.

For hand embroidery, six stranded embroidery floss has been used. Most stitches are worked with two or three strands. When couching, the thread that is being couched down is generally thicker than the thread that you are stitching with. Try six strands, or use a thicker thread such as cotton pearl.

Marker Pencils
There are a variety of marker pens and pencils available designed specifically for fabric. Water soluble pens wash out with a machine wash. Ink pens mark your work permanently, so should never be used.

Sewing Machine
A basic sewing machine with a straight stitch and zigzag is all you need to complete any of the projects in this book. A zipper foot is essential for the Steamer Bag project and making cushions with a piped edge. A buttonhole foot is useful for the Bunny Rucksack and the Sleepy Bear Pyjama Case.

Scissors
Sharp sewing scissors are essential for cutting. Scissors should have long blades, and preferably a bent handle. You will need a pair of paper scissors for cutting out templates; never cut paper with your sewing scissors as this will dull the blades. Embroidery scissors, which have fine pointed blades are ideal for trimming loose ends and clipping into the seam allowance close to your work.

Rotary Cutter
A rotary cutter is shaped like a pizza cutter, with a round rotating blade. It is an excellent tool for cutting through several layers of fabric at one time, for cutting strips, straightening edges and cutting geometric shapes. It must be used with a "self healing" cutting mat, a ruler and a drafting triangle.

Iron

An iron is essential for pressing and setting seams and should be kept close to your work. Keep the plate clean so it does not mark your work. Use a steam or dry iron and press as you go. Each time you stitch a seam, press it.

When pressing appliqué designs or other decorative areas, use a pressing cloth to avoid damage to the fabric. Use a dry iron and a damp pressing cloth for iron-on Pellon interfacings.

SEWING AIDS

Tearaway Stabilizer

Tearaway stabilizers are designed to improve stitch quality. Place under the fabric motif before sewing to the fabric. Stitch through the fabric and the tearaway stabilizer to keep stitches firm and the fabric from puckering. Tearaway stabilizer can be placed on top of the work and stitched over—useful for obtaining good quality satin stitch on fabrics such as terry cloth. Tear away when the stitching is completed.

Fusible Webbing

Fusible webbing has one rough, slightly tacky side and one smooth, peel-off paper side. Place the template right side up on the paper side and trace an outline. Cut the shape. With a hot iron, fuse the webbing to the wrong side of the fabric for ten seconds. Allow to cool, then peel off the paper backing to reveal a flimsy, translucent, slightly tacky surface. Position the shape on the wrong side of the fabric, tacky side down, and with a hot iron, bond the shape to the fabric for five seconds.

Interfacing

When using fusible or iron-on Pellon, press for 15 seconds with a damp cloth.

Batting

Batting is available in a variety of choices, from 100% cotton to 100% polyester, and comes in different weights. Small projects require only 2oz batting. A thick, heavy batting will give a more pronounced quilted effect than thin batting. Fusible fleece batting is available as an alternative.

Buttons

Many projects use buttons for eyes and other decorative features. If the child for whom the project is being made is too young for button decorations, substitute with appliqué shapes or embroidery.

FABRIC

All the measurements given for each project are based on a fabric width of 44–45in/111.8–114.3cm.

Choosing Your Fabric

Many of the projects included in this book are small and require only tiny amounts of fabric. Experienced stitchers may have scraps to hand from previous projects, but for beginners looking to start their first project, buying fat quarters (18 x 22in/45.7 x 55.9cm squares) or remnants from craft and fabric shops is often an ideal way to start.

When buying fabric for the larger projects such as the Playmat or Owl Quilt, take the following points into consideration.

• In choosing a color scheme, look at the room in which the project will be situated and try to coordinate your colors accordingly. Select the colors also with the recipient in mind. Children like bright, clear colors.

• Fabrics that are made of 100% cotton and are dress weight are easiest to work with. They accept fabric markers, are easy to cut, cut with a clean line and sew without fraying. Cotton fabrics can withstand wear and tear, making them an ideal choice for younger children. Cotton washes and irons well, without distorting.

• If you are using dark and light colors together, wash the colors separately before you start, to ensure that the darker shades are colorfast.

107

- If making a quilt or similar project, the backing fabric should be the same fabric type and weight as the front panel to ensure even wear and tear. If the quilt is self-bound and the backing fabric is to be brought to the front of the quilt as a binding, choose a backing color that will coordinate.

CUTTING

Before marking and cutting, square up the raw edges of the fabric piece.

1 Lay the fabric out on a clean, flat surface with a selvage nearest to you and the raw edges facing out. Smooth out any wrinkles.

2 Align a short, straight edge of a drafting triangle with the selvage and with the diagonal edge facing the center of the fabric. Place the long straight edge of the triangle to the right-hand raw edge.

3 Place a ruler against the triangle and hold it down tightly with your left hand. With a fabric marker, draw a straight line along the raw edge of the fabric.

4 Cut along the marked line with scissors or a rotary cutter.

To Cut Strips

1 Fold the fabric in two, with the selvages together.

2 Measure and mark parallel lines the width stated in your pattern.

3 Pin the widths together to prevent the fabric from shifting.

4 Cut along the marked lines.

Rotary Cutting

For the quilts and larger projects requiring long strips of fabric, you may choose to work with a rotary cutter for ease and speed.

1 Place the self healing mat on a hard flat working surface.

2 Fold the fabric in two, right sides facing and selvages matching. Smooth out any creases. Place the drafting triangle on the fold and place a ruler along the straight edge of the triangle parallel with the

selvage. Remove the triangle without moving the ruler. Holding the ruler firmly in place, position the cutter against the edge of the ruler and run the blade away from you without ever losing contact with the ruler.

To cut larger lengths, fold the whole fabric piece, aligning the cut edges. Press. The rotary cutter can cut through eight layers of fabric, so continue to press and fold, until the length of fabric has been used.

Either use your quilter's ruler as a guide to strip widths, or measure and mark your required widths on the fabric, then cut on the lines using the edge of your ruler as a guide.

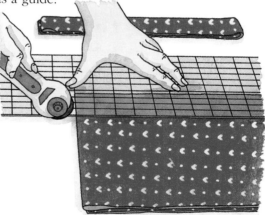

MAKING AND USING TEMPLATES

All the projects contain some element of appliqué work which will necessitate making templates.

1 Using tracing paper and a well-sharpened pencil, trace the outlines of the patterns provided. Cut out and glue the tracing to paper or cardboard. If a template is needed many times over, use template plastic.

2 Cut out the outline to create the template.

3 Place the template right side up on the right side of the fabric and mark an outline with a fabric marker. If you need a back and a front for any of the shapes, flip the template over and mark the reverse outline.

4 Cut out the shape adding a ¼ in/0.6cm seam allowance around all the edges.

STITCHES

MACHINE STITCHES

Work a test sample of the stitches on all your fabric types to ensure the length and width of the stitches are appropriate for the fabric, are comfortable to work with and produce a neat finish. The tension of the top and bottom stitches should be even. Try adjusting the dial/control while the machine is running until you find the best position.

Straight Stitch

Straight stitch is the standard machine sewing stitch. Set your machine stitch length to 2.5 and width to 0.

Zigzag/Overcasting

A wide zigzag is used for tidying or overcasting edges. Try a width of 4 and stitch length of 0.5 or 1.

Satin Stitch

Machine satin stitch is used for appliqué work. It produces a neat and clean outline to fabric shapes. The stitches should be closely worked and cover the raw edge of the motif. In working a sample, try to turn corners and curved edges as well as straight lines. Fine and thick threads react differently to the same settings.

For a wide satin stitch try a stitch width of 4 and length of 0. For a narrow satin stitch, try a width of 2–2.5 and a length of 0.

HAND STITCHES (*see page 114 for illustrations*)

Basting

Basting stitches are temporary stitches worked using a long milliner's needle with basting thread. Work large stitches, ¼in/0.6cm long in a straight line, at an equal distance from the raw edge of the fabric. The length of the stitch should be equal to the length of space between the stitches. Basting stitches form a guideline for machine or hand stitching.

Running Stitch and Gathering Stitch

Running stitch is used for sewing seams. In many of the projects in this book it is also used decoratively. It is worked as for basting stitch, using embroidery floss and smaller stitches. The stitch length and the space between the stitches should be equal.

Slipstitch

Slipstitch is a tiny, invisible stitch, used to hold fabric layers together as in appliqué or in securing a binding. With your needle catch a thread from the bottom fabric, then take a single thread from the top fabric layer.

Backstitch

Usually worked in a straight line and for seams that are liable to heavy wear. Work one running stitch and bring the needle up for a second stitch. Take the needle back down at the end of the first stitch. The stitches are continuous on the right side of the fabric but underneath the stitches overlap.

Blanket Stitch/Buttonhole Stitch

Used for edgings and decoration. Ensure the stitch is straight and the loop lays flat along the edge of the fabric piece.

Buttonhole stitches are worked much closer together than blanket stitch.

Stab Stitch

Use stab stitch when you are working through heavy fabrics and many layers. Work a small straight stitch, pushing the needle through the fabric at a 90 degree angle. Work one stitch at a time.

109

French Knot
Take your needle up through your fabric, and working in a clockwise direction, wrap the thread tightly around the needle once, close to the point. Insert the needle back through the fabric very close to the starting point. Pull the thread though the fabric and the loop on the needle to leave a tight knot close to the surface.

Couching
Lay the thread to be couched in position on the background fabric. With the same color or a contrasting floss, make small stitches at even intervals over the laid floss.

Stem Stitch
A line stitch which creates a fine rope effect.

Satin Stitch
A surface stitch. The stitches are worked tightly together so that no background fabric shows through.

Ladder Stitch
Like slipstitch, ladder stitch is an invisible stitch used to sew two edges together.

APPLIQUÉ
Appliqué means layering or applying one fabric to another. Two methods of appliqué, conventional and bonding using fusible webbing are listed below. Before beginning, try a small sample of each type to establish your preferred method of working.

Bonding Using Fusible Webbing
Note: For raw edge appliqué or machine appliqué do not cut a seam allowance.

1 If you hand stitch your appliqué motifs, after cutting out your fabric shape, clip the seam allowance at right angles to the marked pencil line and fold under the ¼in/0.6cm seam on all the cut out shapes.

2 Place the templates right side up on the paper side of the fusible webbing and mark an outline. Cut each shape on the pencil line.

3 Place the fabric shape right side down on the ironing board with the webbing shape, tacky side down on top. With a hot iron, fuse the two together for ten seconds, then allow to cool.

4 If a motif is made up of several parts, assemble the pieces away from the background fabric to ensure the pieces are placed in the correct order. Position the lower pieces first, and work up to the top pieces.

5 Remove the paper backing and position the pieces on the background fabric. With a hot iron, press the pieces in place. Once bonded to the background, the shapes will not come free, so ensure that they are correctly positioned to begin with.

6 Secure each shape to the background using slipstitch, blanket stitch, or a machine satin stitch.

Conventional Appliqué
1 Clip around the seam allowance at right angles to the marked shape outline. Clipping allows the fabric to be more flexible and creates a neater curved edge. However, if the shapes are large and the curves smooth, clipping is not necessary. Do not breach the seam line.

2 Pin the piece in place on the background fabric.

3 Using the needle or the tip of your finger, push small sections of the seam allowance under the shape as you work your way around.

4 Slipstitch the pieces in place catching in a few strands of the shape and the background fabric.

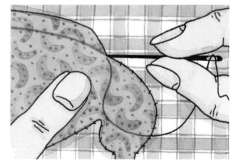

· TEMPLATES/PATTERNS ·

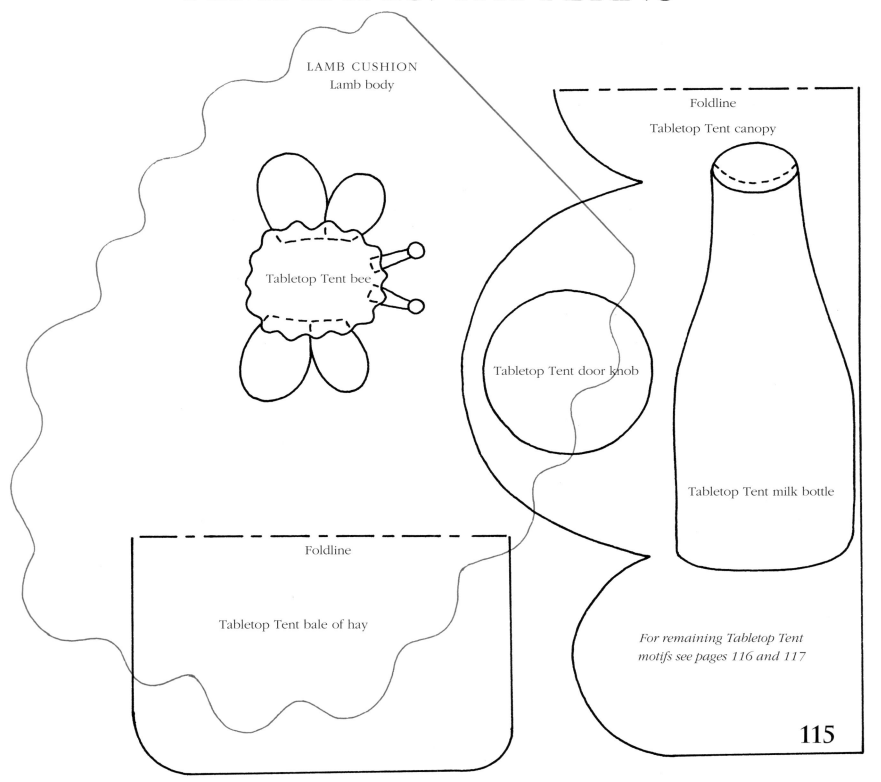

LAMB CUSHION
Lamb body

Foldline
Tabletop Tent canopy

Tabletop Tent bee

Tabletop Tent door knob

Tabletop Tent milk bottle

Foldline

Tabletop Tent bale of hay

For remaining Tabletop Tent motifs see pages 116 and 117

115

Cut 6

116

For remaining motifs see pages 115 and 117

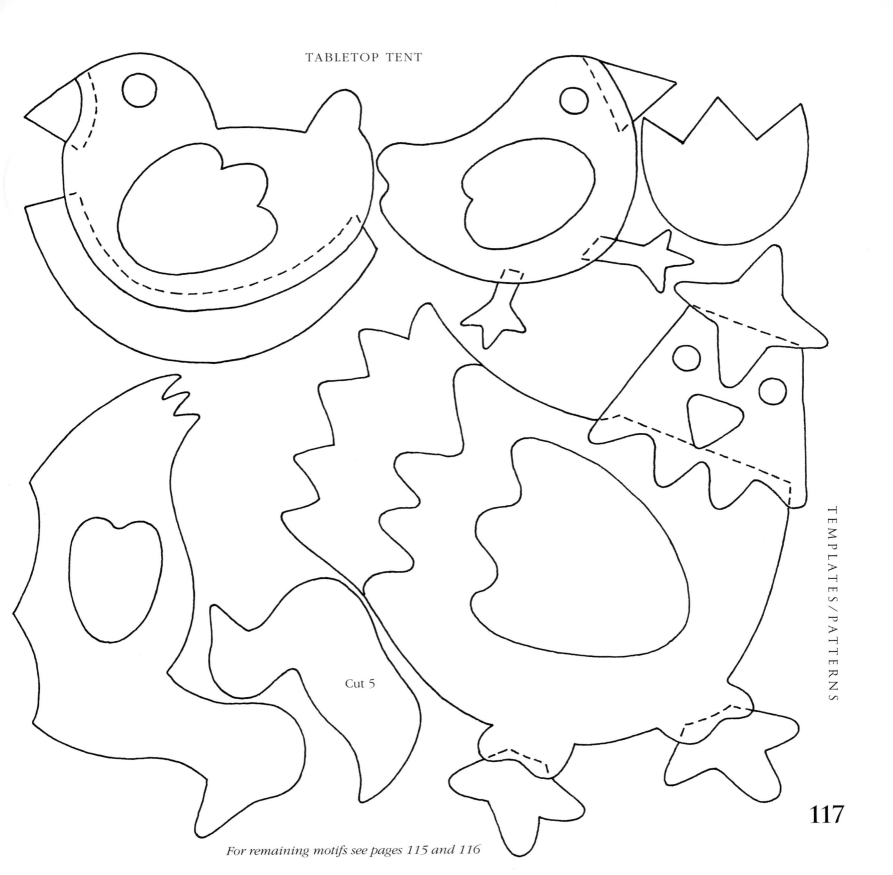

Cut 5

117

For remaining motifs see pages 115 and 116

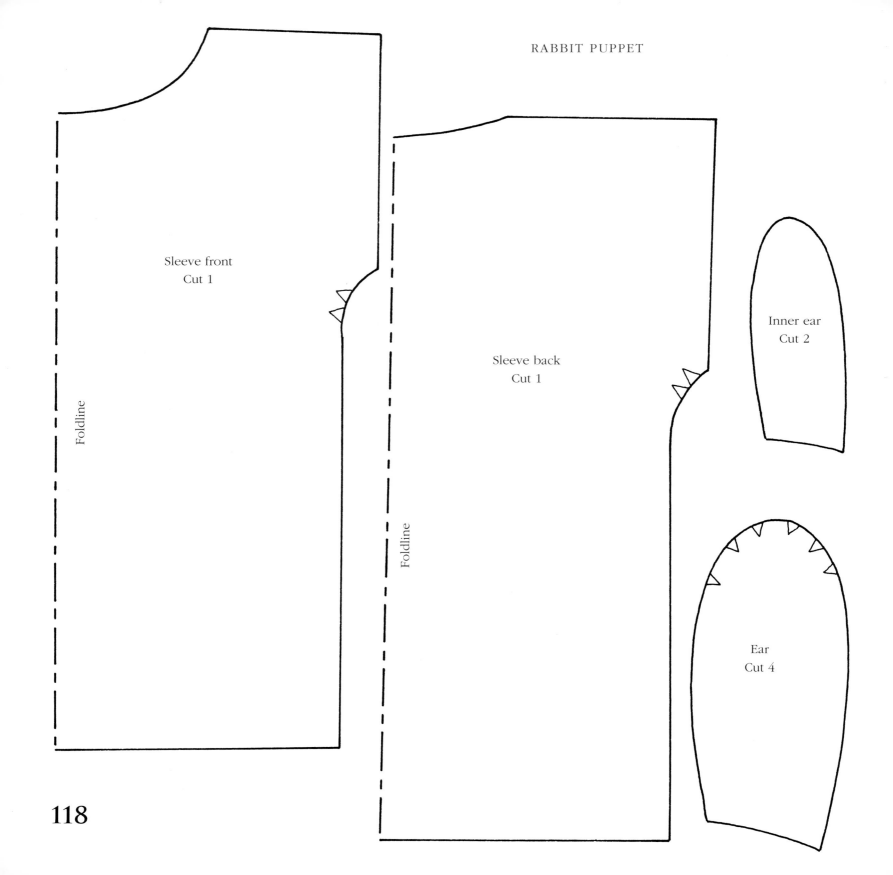

Sleeve front
Cut 1

Foldline

Sleeve back
Cut 1

Foldline

Inner ear
Cut 2

Ear
Cut 4

118

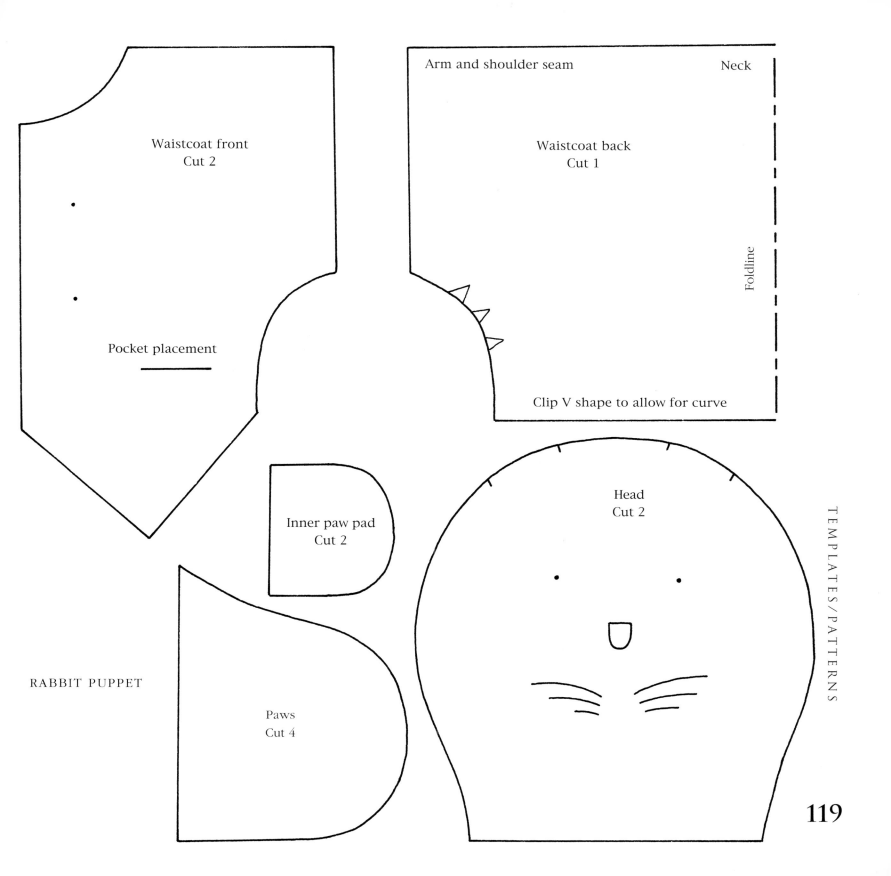

Waistcoat front
Cut 2

Pocket placement

Arm and shoulder seam   Neck

Waistcoat back
Cut 1

Foldline

Clip V shape to allow for curve

Inner paw pad
Cut 2

Head
Cut 2

RABBIT PUPPET

Paws
Cut 4

119

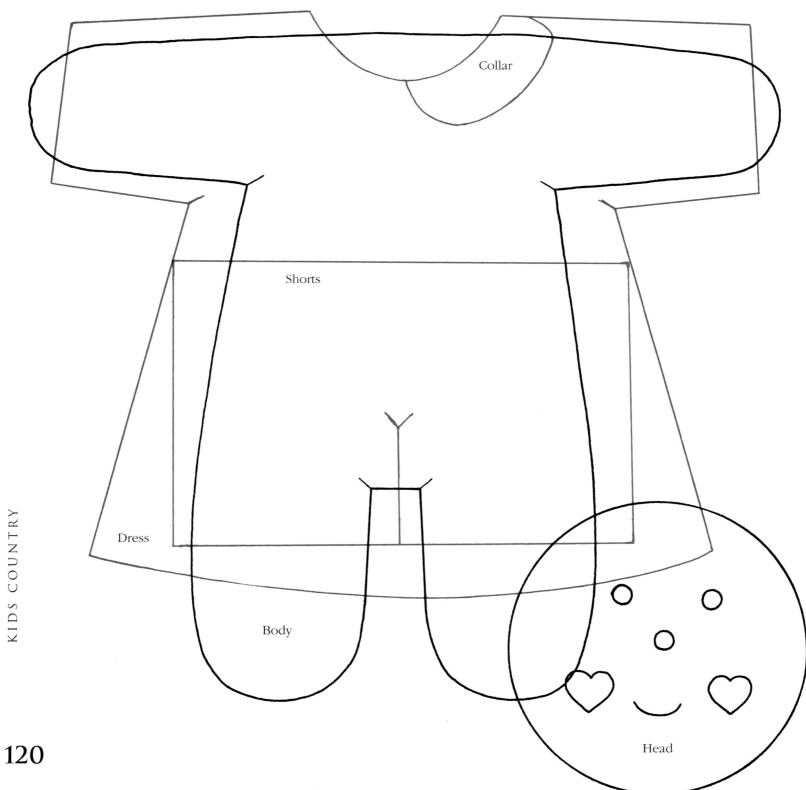

Collar

Shorts

Dress

Body

Head

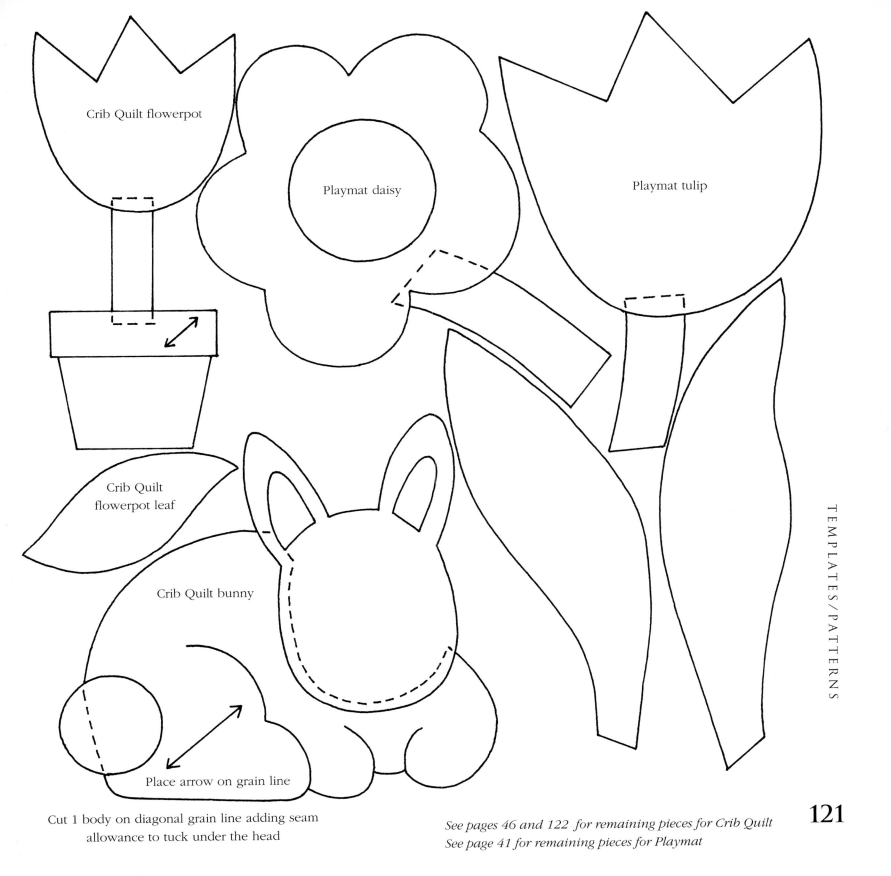

Crib Quilt flowerpot

Playmat daisy

Playmat tulip

Crib Quilt
flowerpot leaf

Crib Quilt bunny

Place arrow on grain line

Cut 1 body on diagonal grain line adding seam
allowance to tuck under the head

See pages 46 and 122 for remaining pieces for Crib Quilt
See page 41 for remaining pieces for Playmat

121

TEMPLATES/PATTERNS

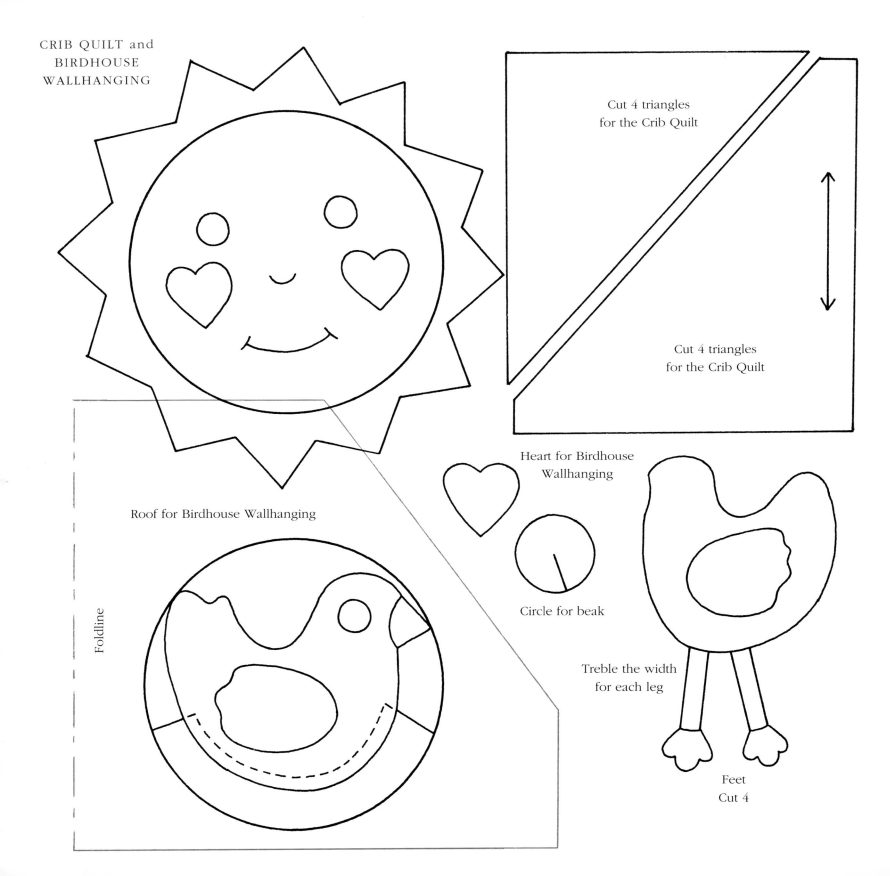

CRIB QUILT and
BIRDHOUSE
WALLHANGING

Cut 4 triangles
for the Crib Quilt

Cut 4 triangles
for the Crib Quilt

Roof for Birdhouse Wallhanging

Foldline

Heart for Birdhouse
Wallhanging

Circle for beak

Treble the width
for each leg

Feet
Cut 4

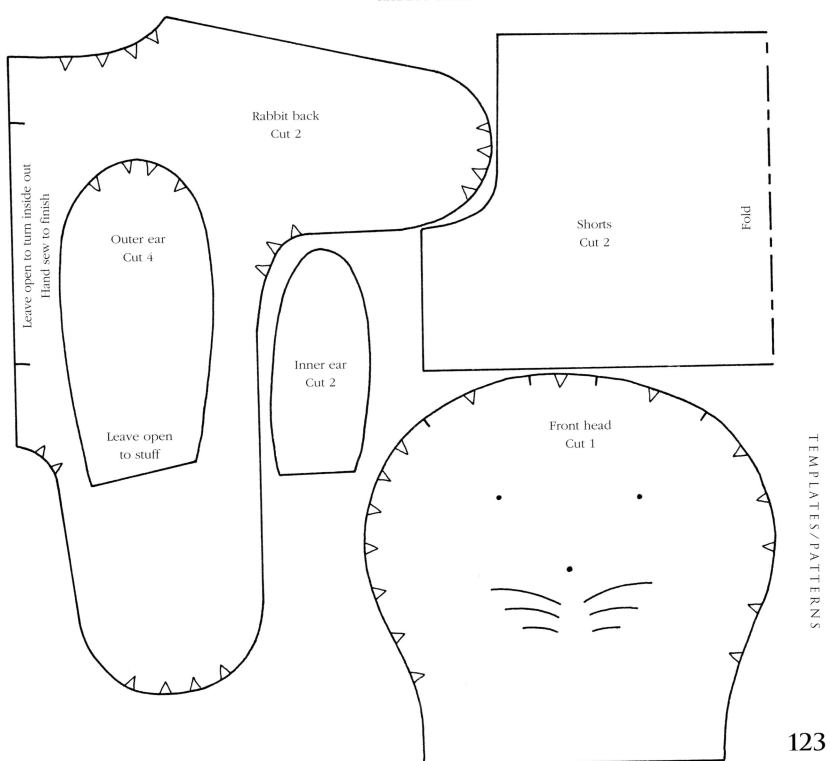

Rabbit back
Cut 2

Leave open to turn inside out
Hand sew to finish

Outer ear
Cut 4

Leave open
to stuff

Inner ear
Cut 2

Shorts
Cut 2

Fold

Front head
Cut 1

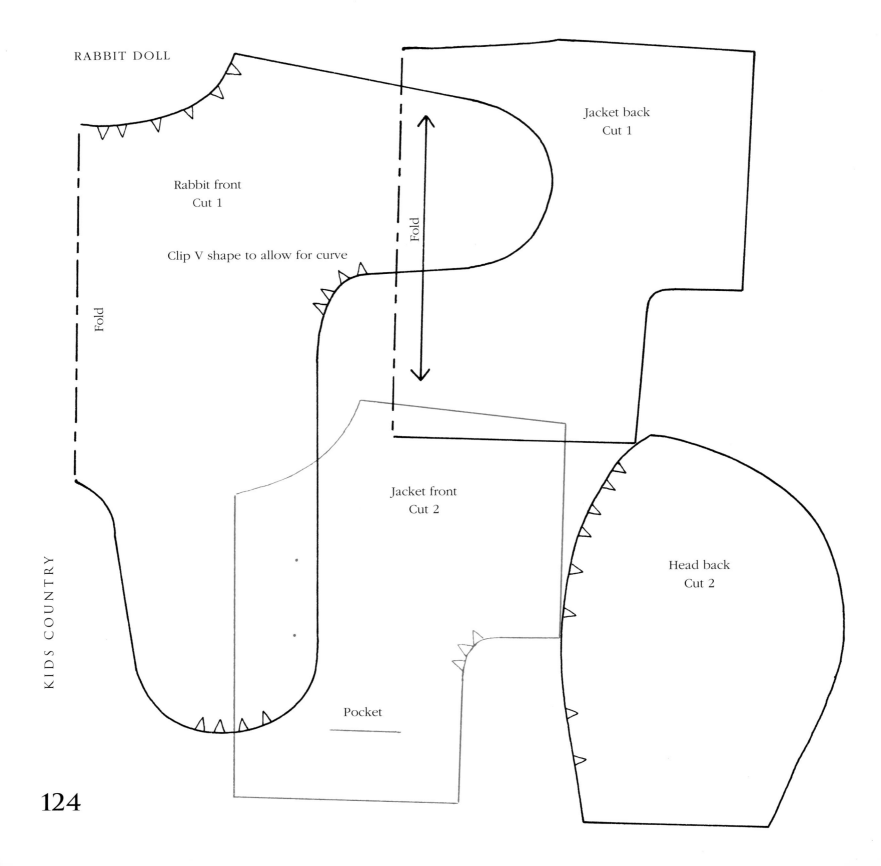

RABBIT DOLL

Rabbit front
Cut 1

Clip V shape to allow for curve

Fold

Fold

Jacket back
Cut 1

Jacket front
Cut 2

Head back
Cut 2

Pocket

KIDS COUNTRY

124

Dotted line denotes seam

For strawberry dish draw a 5in/12.7cm circle
For gingerbread man, draw one circle 4 ½ in/11.4cm and one circle 5in/12.7cm
For remaining Cloth Book motifs see page 59

125

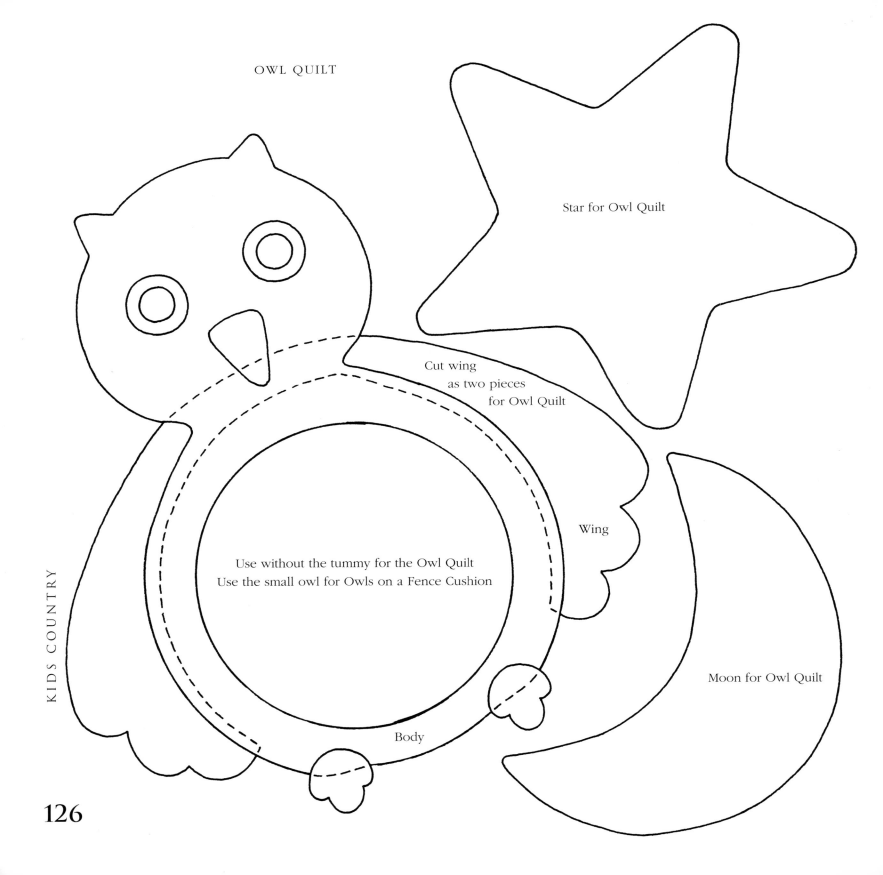

OWL QUILT

Star for Owl Quilt

Cut wing
as two pieces
for Owl Quilt

Wing

Use without the tummy for the Owl Quilt
Use the small owl for Owls on a Fence Cushion

Moon for Owl Quilt

KIDS COUNTRY

Body

126

PIG AND
RABBIT BAGS

Dotted line denotes seam

Pig's
shoulders

Cut 3 carrots

Stem

Leaf

Top

Apple

127

· INDEX ·